Role Playing:
A Practical Manual
for Group Facilitators

by
Malcolm E. Shaw
Raymond J. Corsini
Robert R. Blake
Jane S. Mouton

University Associates, Inc.
8517 Production Avenue
San Diego, California 92121

Copyright © 1980 by International Authors, B.V.

ISBN: 0-88390-156-0

Library of Congress Catalog Card Number: 79-67712

Printed in the United States of America

Table of Contents

Introduction

The term "role playing" represents at least four distinct concepts:

1. *Theatrical.* An actor plays a role as defined by the playwright and the director. The actor repeats certain words and actions in a predetermined manner.
2. *Sociological.* This refers to the usual behavior of people in particular societies—how they act under certain circumstances in formal ways. It is used in the sense that all social behavior represents a playing of culturally determined patterns.
3. *Dissimulative.* People play roles with the intention of deceiving or of creating impressions contrary to their real feelings. The spy in enemy territory and the employee who is polite to a disliked superior are playing roles.
4. *Educational.* The subject of this book is an action-spontaneity procedure that takes place under contrived circumstances. It has three general purposes: (a) diagnosing—to provide better understanding of the role players by seeing and hearing them in action; (b) informing—to give the observers information about how certain roles should be filled; and (c) training—to provide the role players with knowledge and skills by permitting them to experience a nearly real situation and to provide feedback information to help them better understand themselves and their behavior.

Educational role playing is a skill and, like any skill, must be practiced in order to be learned or mastered. The surgeon, before he can operate, must observe other surgeons and serve a long apprenticeship. The concert pianist rehearses for many weary hours before appearing on the stage. Role playing is one of the few ways in which one can practice the complicated and all-important human relations skills of leading, managing, and coordinating people.

Role playing is reality practice and action learning; it involves realistic behavior under unrealistic conditions. The boxer who spars with his shadow is role playing; the lawyer who argues a case before friends or family is role playing; the executive who practices a speech in front of a secretary is role playing. The doing of something as though it were "for real" enhances those skills—this is "practice."

Of course, some human relations skills can be learned by reading books, listening to lectures, or watching films. Role playing, however, is a much more effective manner of learning complex skills because it repeats and reinforces the accomplishment of those skills. This is frequently called "learning by doing." In role playing one thinks, feels, and acts at the same time; one is involved comprehensively and globally in the situation. Too often in life we know what to do but cannot do it, either because of fear or other emotional hindrances or because we just do not have the skills. There is no difference in essence between learning to fly an airplane and learning to handle a labor dispute; both may be learned by watching others through lectures and books, but it is only through experience that one can really learn to do the task adequately. One important aspect of role playing is that it *provides a simulated reality experience in which one can practice complex skills without hurting oneself or anyone else through failure.*

Role playing has many purposes; four specific ones that are addressed in this book are:

1. *Informing.* When group members are watching and listening and not role playing themselves, role playing is then used for informing, and the role players become living audiovisual teaching aids.
2. *Training.* All procedures with the objective of improving skills can be called training. For example, if a new salesperson role plays a difficult sales situation and the purpose is to learn how to meet such a situation in real life, this is training. He or she is "learning by doing."
3. *Evaluating.* When the purpose of role playing is to analyze and evaluate the role player, the procedure is done for evaluation.
4. *Modifying Behavior.* When the role play is used as a stimulus to evoke a response (new patterns of acting) and to practice and reinforce the response, it is a behavior-modification technique.

PURPOSE OF THE BOOK

This book is intended to serve as an introduction to role playing. It is directed to people concerned with the development of human relations skills, selling, interviewing, teaching, handling grievances, counseling, supervising, etc. Much of this material is useful in other areas such as community affairs and commercial enterprises; in both of these settings role playing has been used with good results.

This book is based substantially on an earlier work by Corsini, Shaw, and Blake, *Roleplaying in Business and Industry*. It has been updated, new sections have been added, and much of the content has been revised.

The authors have assumed various responsibilities for parts of the book, but it is a collaboration, since each part has been read, revised, edited, and approved by all the authors. Since we have considerably different experiences and points of view in this field, we present not just a single approach but the consensus of our thinking.

Blake and Mouton were responsible for the first section, *Background*. This section contains the history, theory, and general implications of role playing. It provides a frame of reference for understanding the meaning and purpose of role playing.

The second section, *Techniques*, written by Shaw and Corsini, deals with a variety of action role-playing procedures. It tells the beginner how to proceed and what to guard against in role playing.

The third section, *Applications*, was the responsibility of Shaw. This part concerns itself with the various uses of role playing. It explains how and for what purposes role playing can be used. Chapter 9, Evaluating, is primarily by Corsini. Chapter 10, Modifying Behavior, is by Shaw.

The *Appendixes*, prepared by Corsini, consist of structured situations that the beginning role-play director will find useful and observer recording forms. An *Annotated Bibliography* of role playing in industry and allied areas will suggest further reading and applications.

We hope the reader will use this volume as a springboard for creative role playing. Like the interview, role playing is a simple technique whose possibilities no one shall ever master completely. We believe that it has exciting, profitable potential. No trainer or group leader should be without a basic understanding of the meaning, purposes, values, and potential of role playing. If we have been of help in pointing these out, our efforts are well repaid.

Malcom E. Shaw,
Raymond J. Corsini,
Robert R. Blake,
Jane S. Mouton

BACKGROUND

1

The Origins and Uses of Role Playing

Role playing is a method of learning about human interaction that involves realistic behavior in imaginary situations. It is a *spontaneous* technique, since participants act freely rather than from a script. Although the situation in which the interaction takes place is contrived, the role players act as though what they are doing is "for real." The major purposes of role playing are (a) to provide training for skills in dealing with information or insights into the nature of human behavior and (b) to provide evaluation of and feedback to people relative to increasing their effectiveness in various situations.

THE ORIGINS OF ROLE PLAYING

It is likely that role playing was first used as a teaching and learning method long ago, perhaps the first time an employer said to an apprentice, "Pretend I am a customer, and show how you would treat me." If the two stopped now and then to discuss, evaluate, and practice alternative ways of interacting or reacting, they role played.

A Viennese psychiatrist, J. L. Moreno, was the originator (Moreno, 1923) of the modern concept of role playing, and his writings present the rationale for and methods of role playing. Moreno maintained that emotional problems could be corrected if people acted out troubling situations and analyzed and practiced new solutions. To do this, he employed a complex version of role playing, known as *psychodrama*.

In 1933, the German Army, limited to 100,000 men by the terms of the Versailles Treaty, began to develop a corps of officers. For the selection of military personnel, Simoneit (1933), a German military psychologist, devised a number of action procedures very similar to current role playing by which officers could estimate the qualities of army recruits. After the fall of Dunkirk, the British Army employed similar procedures in its officer-slection program (Davies, 1956). In the United States, the Office of Strategic Services Assessment Staff (1948) used role playing in the selection of people for secret wartime work.

Role playing began to be used in the United States for teaching purposes during World War II, with early reports of its use in industrial training by Lippitt (1943) and French (1945). Later discussions of role playing are by Argyris (1951), Corsini (1957, 1966), and Starr (1977).

Generally, role playing now is recognized as a valuable procedure whenever people need to understand a situation better or be more effective in dealing with it.

THE USES OF ROLE PLAYING

Training

Perhaps the most important use of role playing is for training. Role playing gives insight into the skills necessary for dealing with various interpersonal situations (see Hundleby & Zingle, 1975) and can be useful in training for any job that involves human interaction. It also can be used to help people improve specific (e.g., on-the-job) skills. An individual may be asked to demonstrate how he handles a certain situation. Discussion and analysis follow, including suggestions from the facilitator and the group about how the performance can be improved. The trainee may try the role again, making an effort to vary the procedure, or may watch others demonstrate how they handle the role.

Example: An employee has been hired as a new accounts representative in a bank. The new employee has no previous experience in this type of work. A role-play situation is set up in which the employee handles a potential new account. By acting out the situation, discussing and evaluating the interaction, and then trying out alternative ways of attempting it, the new employee receives training and practice in the skills of client service.

Example: A salesman is in a slump; sales have been falling off, and advice and encouragement have not helped. A role-play situation involving a salesman and a prospect is set up. The salesman plays his own role, going through the scene several times. Observers tell him that he acts hesitantly and seems ill at ease. The salesman may not believe this. Someone else then acts out the role as he saw the salesman act it. The salesman protests that it is a crude distortion of how he acted, but the others assure him that the portrayal is correct. They also demonstrate other approaches for him to try. He then re-enacts the role, trying to handle it in a different way, or he plays the part of the prospect while someone else plays his role.

Role playing is well suited for training in human relations (see Teahan, 1975) because playing the role of another person forces one to put oneself in the other's place, to feel and behave as the other person would. A successful role play increases one's understanding of others involved in the situation.

Role playing also is helpful in encouraging changes in behavior. It is well known that there can be a discrepancy between one's knowledge and one's behavior (see Argyris, 1976) and that old habits are difficult to change.

Example: A mother reports to her group that she has difficulty getting her daughter to keep her room neat. Rather than giving advice or suggesting rules or punishment, the group asks the mother to role play a typical confrontation with another person playing the role of the daughter. When the members of the group see the mother's approach, they suggest alternative approaches that might be more effective in soliciting her daughter's cooperation. The mother then re-enacts the scene, trying one alternative approach, receiving suggestions about how she may implement it better, and then evaluating it in terms of what its probable effect might be with her daughter. The mother can then try the new approach(es) in seeking to solve the problem with her daughter.

Example: A person may be told that the use of sarcasm is a poor technique for influencing others. He may even accept this idea but continue to use sarcasm. If he takes part in a role play and becomes aware of the effects of his sarcasm on others or if he watches another person act and talk as he himself usually does, the effects of sarcasm may be vividly impressed upon him. The possibility of change and alternative behavior is much increased.

Communication

Information frequently must be transmitted from one source, an expert, to another, a novice or pupil. However, unless the "expert" is also skilled in communication, the information may not be transmitted in a way that enables others to understand or grasp it.

The most usual format for such direct transmission of knowledge is the lecture. It is most effective if the audience can *see* or visualize mentally what is being discussed and if the lecturer uses gestures, tone of voice, rhetorical questions, and other techniques to hold the interest of the audience.

Role playing, since it helps to implant messages firmly, can be used to help persons improve their communication skills in order to transmit information effectively.

Example: A classroom teacher in a summer workshop with other teachers indicates that she feels her students are less interested in the topic than she had anticipated. Her colleagues ask her to enact a typical presentation as she would in her classroom (see Ettkin & Snyder, 1972).

In discussing her presentation, the other teachers describe it as a monolog which, though well outlined, would offer the students no opportunity to ask questions or to test the implications of what has been presented. Furthermore, the teacher failed to summarize, and the students would not be aided in digesting the material she had presented. After this critique the teacher makes a second effort to present the material in a more stimulating and involving way and is more effective in doing so.

Similarly, medical students can be helped to communicate better with patients, lawyers with clients, real estate agents with prospects, or scientists with government administrators who do not have technical knowledge.

Using role playing for communication is of value particularly when changes in attitude and behavior are desired. Shaw (1956) has given examples and evaluated role playing as an approach to job instruction.

Example: The management of a company has decided on a policy change that affects all employees. A meeting is called with all supervisors since it is essential that they understand the reasons for the change so they can interpret it correctly to their employees.

The chairman of the meeting introduces a role play with several people acting the part of management while the supervisors look on. The role-play discussion concerns the policy change, and the pros and cons are debated. The supervisors are thus presented the reasons for the change. They predict a negative attitude and decide that supervisors must be apprised of the importance of this new policy (see Johnson & Dustin, 1970).

Two people are then called on to play the roles of an executive and a supervisor. They discuss the change in policy; then the "supervisor" talks to some "employees," who raise objections to the change. The "supervisor" finally convinces them of its value.

In this manner, the *real* supervisors in the audience are instructed about the problem in a dramatic manner. They hear possible objections of employees and, more important, they see the ways in which they may be able to meet and overcome such objections. The effect of such a role play depends on the meaningfulness of the drama to the members of the audience.

Evaluation

Governments, schools, businesses, and other institutions depend on accurate evaluation in order to select personnel, analyze training needs, determine operational changes, and so on. However, in dealing with human relations situations or problems, it often is hard to obtain valued or reliable information. Role playing can be of considerable value for this purpose. Observers see and hear a person in action in a simulated but psychologically real situation. They can learn from the person's reactions and can also provide input on how the situation can be handled better.

Example: A candidate for the job of door-to-door salesman is asked to role play a typical selling situation in order to evaluate the candidate's sales ability. This kind of role playing is a test; it provides a *sample* of the candidate's behavior in a particular situation.

Possibly the best application of role-play methods for evaluation and assessment is the assessment-center concept. This is an organized procedure in which standard performances are evaluated by trained observers or experts; it may be significant in determining a person's career progress. Assessment-center technique was brought to a high state of sophistication by Bray (1966), who for many years experimentally evaluated its efficiency for this purpose at American Telephone and Telegraph (Bray, 1974). It has now come into permanent use at AT&T as well as in such organizations as IBM, Caterpillar, General Electric, Sears, Westinghouse, and Macy's department store, and in numerous government agencies and school systems. (See Cohen, Moses, & Byham, 1972; DiCostanzo & Andretta, 1970; and Lawton, 1975.)

Role playing also can be used to determine effective or ineffective ways of handling certain operations or assignments.

Example: Three people in the personnel department of a large organization do the same kind of interviewing. They all seem to do the job equally well. Brown typically interviews seven people a day, Jones, eleven, and Smith, fifteen. Their supervisor would like to bring Brown and Jones up to Smith's level of efficiency. To do so, the supervisor would like to find out what typical procedures are used by each of the three people.

Direct observation of each interviewer might be unwise, since it could change the relationship between the interviewer and the interviewee. A more practical method is to have Brown, Jones, and Smith each role play an interviewing situation. Observers would use a check list to evaluate each role play. If Smith maintains efficiency over Brown and Jones in the role-play tests, the other two might be asked to evaluate Smith's methods and then try to make use of them.

For instance, Brown and Jones may use procedures that are not necessary, e.g., spending a good deal of time trying to establish rapport with the interviewee. Smith may proceed more quickly to the business at hand. Through role playing, many inefficient practices can be spotted and eliminated.

Role playing also may be used to evaluate and improve supervisory practices.

Example: Morale is low in a particular department, and the source of the problem evidently is the foreman. He is interested in finding out what causes his troubles. Before observers he role plays typical on-the-job situations. Through discussions with the observers, he begins to recognize what is ineffective in his dealings with employees. Additional practice permits him to use the skills needed to increase his effectiveness.

Role playing can be used for numerous other types of evaluation. It has an advantage over alternative procedures (questionnaires, tests, interviews, data sheets, etc.) in that it is *here and now, natural,* and *spontaneous.* It provides observers with direct material that is pertinent to the evaluation and not distorted by errors in communication (common to other procedures). Borgatta (1956) who investigated the relative value of diagnostic tests and role playing, reported role playing to be more accurate than paper-and-pencil tests for the prediction of human behavior.

SUMMARY

Role playing is a spontaneous human interaction that involves realistic behavior enacted in imaginary situations for purposes of learning. Role playing as a learning tool came into prominence after World War II; its use has been dramatically expanded in the 1960s and 1970s. The technique has an endless variety of applications for training, developing communication skills, and evaluation.

REFERENCES

Argyris, C. *Role playing in action.* New York State School of Industrial and Labor Relations, Cornell University. Bulletin No. 16, May 1951.

Argyris, C. Theories in action that inhibit individual learning. *American Psychologist,* 1975, *31,* 638-654.

Borgatta, E. F. Analysis of social interaction: Actual, role playing and projective. *Journal of Abnormal and Social Psychology,* 1956, *40,* 190-196.

Bray, D. W., Campbell, R. J., & Grant, D. L. *Formative years in business: A long-term AT&T study of managerial lives.* New York: John Wiley, 1974.

Bray, D. W., & Grant, D. L. The assessment center in the measurement of potential for business management. *Psychological Monographs,* 1966, 80(17, Whole No. 625).

Cohen, B. M., Moses, J. L., & Byham, W. C. *The validity of assessment centers: A literature review.* Pittsburgh, PA: Development Dimensions, 1972.

Corsini, R. J. *The role playing technique in business and industry.* Chicago: Industrial Relations Center. Occasional Paper No. 9, April 1957.

Corsini, R. J. *Roleplaying in psychotherapy: A manual.* Chicago: Aldine, 1966.

Davies, A. T. *Industrial training.* London: Institute of Personnel Management, 1956.

DiCostanzo, F., & Andretta, T. The supervisory assessment center in the Internal Revenue Service. *Training and Development Journal,* September 1970.

Ettkin, L., & Snyder, L. A model for peer group counseling based on role-play. *School Counselor,* 1972, *19,* 215-218.

French, J. R. P. Role playing as a method of training foremen. *Sociometry,* 1945, *8,* 410-422.

Hundleby, G., & Zingle, H. Communication of empathy. *Canadian Counselor,* 1975, *9,* 148-152.

Johnson, D. W., & Dustin, R. The initiation of cooperation through role reversal. *Journal of Social Psychology,* 1970, *82,* 193-203.

Lawton, E. C. Identifying executive potential: Methods of testing and assessing. In B. Taylor & G. L. Lippitt (Eds.), *Management development and training handbook.* London: McGraw-Hill, 1975.

Lippitt, R. The psychodrama in leadership training. *Sociometry,* 1943, *6,* 286-292.

Moreno, J. L. *Das Stegreif Theater.* Potsdam: Kiepenhever, 1923.

Office of Strategic Services Assessment Staff. *Assessment of men.* New York: Holt, Rinehart and Winston, 1948.

Shaw, M.E. Role playing—A procedural approach. *Journal of the American Society of Training Directors,* 1956, *10* (March-April), 23 ff.

Simoneit, M. *Wehr Psychologie.* Charlottenberg: Bernard & Graefe, 1933.

Starr, A. *Rehearsal for living: Psychodrama.* Chicago: Nelson-Hall, 1977.

Teahan, J. E. Role playing and group experience to facilitate attitude and value changes among black and white police officers. *Journal of Social Issues,* 1975, *31*(1). 35-45.

2

The Rationale for Role Playing

A clear explanation of the underlying rationale for role playing can indicate particular advantages for training, communication, and evaluation. At present, there are several distinct approaches to teaching people how to deal more effectively with others. A brief description of these different approaches and methods provides a basis for understanding the unique contribution that role playing makes.

TEACHING METHODS

The Lecture

In the conventional classroom the teacher stands before the students, who are seated. The teacher often speaks from an outline, while the students take notes. Occasionally a question may be asked and answered. Learning is measured by examination. This procedure, more or less typical of traditional classroom teaching, involves a relatively active teacher role and a passive audience.

This classroom method of instruction can be called the "empty container" theory. Students come to the learning situation with receptive but empty minds. The instructor knows what they should learn. His or her task is to present material in an understandable way and, through examinations, to assess the learning that has taken place for each individual. To improve the quality of teaching, the instructor may use a number of aids. One is the textbook, in which lecture material is amplified. Another aid is the chalkboard; if a concept can be diagramed and relationships seen in visual terms, understanding is likely to be improved. A third aid is the use of audiovisual devices to clarify or dramatize important points. The teacher also may assign problems or readings as homework, so that the student applies effort in a constructive way.

For certain types of subject matter, this method is an excellent approach to teaching. When it comes to learning to deal with people, however, the lecture alone rarely helps an individual to be more effective. Knowledge and verbal insight are insufficient to produce changes in individual behavior (see Schmuck, 1969).

A number of variations of teacher-centered learning strengthen the teacher's presentation of concepts, ideas, information, and further the student's understanding.

The Conference

In the conference method the teacher meets with a small group; the shift is from a teacher-centered situation to a give-and-take interaction between the teacher and the students. The development of a topic is likely to be less orderly than in a conventional classroom situation because the give-and-take may lead the conversation in unanticipated directions. Furthermore, in the exchange of thinking that takes place the teacher may realize that it is necessary to backtrack to correct misunderstandings, amplify a previous point, or convey, supplement, or develop implications that need to be understood. In a conference situation, the teacher becomes more than a subject-matter expert; the teacher moves into the role of a facilitator who takes responsibility for ensuring that students have a good level of comprehension of the topic.

The conference method may include supplemental techniques such as the use of small discussion groups when the number of students is so large that it is impractical for everyone to interact spontaneously with the expert. By discussing in small groups what has been presented, learners may gain many of the advantages of direct interaction with the teacher. These small discussion groups are often called "buzz groups."

The limitation of this method, however, is similar to that of the conventional classroom: without enactment, students are expected to acquire an intellectual understanding of the subject but may not necessarily gain a functional appreciation of how to use the knowledge.

Tele-Teaching

Tele-teaching is a technical variation of the conventional classroom method. The conference method and buzz groups can be employed when the expert presentation is made by television. It sometimes is possible with the use of a telephone for students to pose questions directly to the teacher and to get direct answers, as in the conference method.

The Case Method

The case method has rapidly gained in popularity since its inception at the Harvard Business School in the early 1900 s (Dooley & Skinner, 1977). This approach involves writing a "true" situation describing a problem that people are trying to solve and various approaches to its solution that could be considered; it often requires the student to decide a resolution to the problem.

In the case method, the instructor is not an instructor in the conventional sense and deliberately and consistently avoids inserting expert subject matter into the case discussion. The case instructor performs as procedural technician, assigning the case that will be discussed in the next session and then leading the discussion by asking that the main points of the case be summarized. If there is no summary, the instructor then moves directly into a discussion of the pros and cons of the actions taken at various points and of alternative actions that might have been considered and what their implications would have been. Based on this wide-ranging discussion, students diagnose what they think is the real problem and what their approach to its solution might have been.

In the conventional case method, there are no right or wrong answers. The learning comes from giving each student an opportunity to discuss with others how they think and feel about the problem. Each person is thereby able to contrast his or her thoughts about how to best solve the problem with the views that are expressed by others.

The case method induces widespread involvement in the discussion and allows each person to present his or her thinking spontaneously. Furthermore, the case method may be one of the few available teaching techniques that would be tolerated by people who have advanced knowledge or understanding. For example, teachers, lawyers, doctors, or managers who have had years of experience often are amenable to sitting, each with his or her own group, and exploring ideas about how to deal with complex problems, whereas they frequently are not inclined to sit and listen to a presentation that is typical of the conventional classroom situation.

An important variation of the case method is to build theory into the case itself; then after people have explored their "natural" modes of thought relative to the problem, they can test their thinking against what theory would have specified as the optimal solution.

A major limitation of the case method is, again, that it involves verbal levels of interaction, i.e., the learner can acquire verbal understanding and still not have the skills to deal with others who may be involved.

Sensitivity Training

Sensitivity training came into practice just after World War II and has been established as a standard technique for learning about human behavior and about oneself in relation to other people.

In its classical design, sensitivity training involves twelve to fifteen strangers coming together for an extended period of time such as a week or two and for two to four hours a day. The group meets with a trainer who often is called a facilitator.

There is a unique situation among strangers in a sensitivity-training group that is unlikely to occur in other areas of life. The reason is that the facilitator inserts no agenda to help the group get started. As a result, a vacuum is created because the members are unacquainted with one another. They have different experiences and skills. Yet the purpose of the meetings is for them to learn from one another how to be more effective in interacting with others.

Slowly, the vacuum fills, and it is the facilitator's task to invoke the feedback mechanism at various critical points along the way. The facilitator does this by engaging the group in studying its process—*how* it has been doing whatever it has been doing—and thereby aiding people to see such things as why the discussion has evolved in the way it has or why some members are "pushers" and others limit their participation to supporting or merely observing the group.

In the process of filling the vacuum, innumerable human dynamics of competition, cooperation, conflict, creativity, commitment, and so on come to the surface; each of these can be examined to determine what caused it and, if negative, what would correct it.

The sensitivity group is a unique learning experience; it can aid participants in learning very deeply about themselves, their impact on others, and what they might do to strengthen the quality of their social and problem-solving relationships.

Although the sensitivity-training setting is not "real life" in the literal sense of an interaction in a job or family, it is realistic in that people feel the impact of acceptance and rejection from their colleagues. As a result, the sensitivity-training experience draws out genuine, spontaneous behavior, and it is in the analysis of such conduct that benefits can be realized.

Often the sensitivity-training group is supplemented by role playing. The role-play exercise provides a situational problem for participants to enact in order to experience various solutions to it. The stated problem might be how to respond assertively to an angry family member, or how to communicate with another teacher who is being criticized by his or her students and is unaware of it, or how to react to a strong authority figure in a problem-solving rather than a submissive or defensive way. The use of role playing in the context of sensitivity training can enlarge the area of learning by enabling people to experience their own reactions under imaginary conditions. In these circumstances there is little or no secondary consequence in terms of acceptance or rejection from others or of making mistakes for which there would be a penalty, as there might be in real life.

Simulation

The word *simulation* originally meant something that deceives, is an illusion, or is meant to deceive, as a fraud or imposture. Today it is a recognized and respected term, meaning the approximation of certain environmental or other conditions for purposes of training or experimentation. A simulation tests a provisional model or activity against pre-established standards before the actual process occurs. It calls for the active participation of the producers themselves in solving the problems they create. If difficulties are encountered, the causes can be identified and eliminated before they appear in the real situation. Simulation, then, is creating a replica of what is expected to occur (Blake & Mouton, 1978).

There are three broad classes of simulations: dry runs and dress rehearsals, prototypes and pilot projects, and model building.

Dry Runs and Dress Rehearsals. After plans have been made about what should occur in an operational situation, it is possible to implement them on a dry-run basis or to conduct a dress rehearsal to evaluate and debug the plans before the actual situation occurs.

Example: Practicing before a football game is simulation. One team is assigned to replicate the opposition's expected game plan, and the other is coached to overcome the opposition. Then a game itself is played to try offensive and defensive strategies. When the opposition is well programed, a close approximation to actual circumstances in the real game is likely. Corrections can then be introduced into the game strategy and performances of specific players can be evaluated.

Dress rehearsals before a wedding ceremony, a formal rehearsal before a stage play, answering sample test questions before a college examination, mock trials in law school, or pretesting a speech are further examples of this process.

Prototypes and Pilot Projects. There are some discrete activities for which there is little or no prior history. Simulation is one of the problem-solving techniques for moving such an activity from hypothesis to operation. By passing through a pilot-project stage—such as building and operating a pilot plant before constructing one that would be hundreds of times more expensive—it becomes possible to identify unforeseen problems and weaknesses.

A prototype is usually an even more tentative version. It may represent only the key outlines of the project or may be constructed on a miniature scale. A prototype, however, does contain all identified, major variables, positioned to operate as they would in the real case.

Model Building. A third simulation strategy involves identifying the known variables in an actual situation and then setting up a hypothetical model in which those variables are expected to operate. The soundness of a model often can be evaluated after the fact by feeding historical data into it and then determining how well the model predicts what is actually known to have happened. If the model is demonstrated to be accurate, and few, if any, unknown variables are present, the model permits the future to be projected. Consequences can then be anticipated before they occur by examining the model's operation over many years ahead. It thus becomes possible to anticipate what the future is likely to be and to prepare for it in advance. This method of problem solving can be an important basis for learning from hypothetical experience.

This type of model building is probably best known in economics. One example is the Wharton Model[1] for forecasting what the future economy is likely to be, but there are a number of other private, public, and governmental economic models. Model building is also used in technical fields, e.g., to anticipate where to drill for oil or to predict a flu epidemic.

A recent expansion of the use of statistical projection from known parameters is the environmental impact study. When limits and standards for some performance already have been established, e.g., through legislation, any anticipated activity can be evaluated to determine whether its consequences would meet or exceed those limits and standards.

Forrester's (1973) Urban Dynamics model is used to analyze and describe what causes cities to rise and fall. Rather than replicating a whole city as a basis for projecting its future, the Forrester model creates a city from empirical data to learn what its basic functionings are.

One of the better-known applications of simulation is the use of feasibility studies for evaluating an action prior to making a commitment to engage in it. This is, however, a second-best kind of simulation. Many of the variables that operate in the real situation and their probable interaction cannot be anticipated. They frequently have to be ignored or treated as constants. As a result, feasibility studies tend to concentrate excessively on financial variables and to leave out or give superficial attention to marketing and human variables. This explains why the findings of feasibility studies are often very different from the real operations that follow them.

Counseling

Emphasis in individual counseling is mainly on clarifying emotions, feelings, and attitudes. Counseling is a way of stimulating changes in personal behavior. It is a method for repairing personality.

But individual counseling is no answer to the full spectrum of problems of people working together. One reason is that the normal range of human problems is not so "deep" as to require treatment. Personality is only one cause of interpersonal problems, and in many situations it is a relatively unimportant consideration. Another reason is that treatment fails to aid individuals in accommodating to one another successfully when their difficulty stems from factors within the situation itself. For example, the bickering that goes on in many companies between the research and development department and the production department is often cleared up merely by exploring the properties of the situation that contribute to competitiveness and disagreement. A practical solution is not likely

---

[1]Professor Lawrence Klein, of the Wharton School of Business, University of Pennsylvania, is credited with developing the Wharton Model.

to be found merely by evaluating the feelings of the people who are faced with the problem. An effort to counsel hostile individuals in order to render them more friendly and cooperative might ignore the fact that the problem might be built into the situation itself. Similarly, a lecture on the problems of intergroup conflict also would probably do little to solve the problem. Of course, if any person in the situation suffered from personal problems of an extreme nature, psychotherapy might be advised for that person.

The lecture, the conference, the case method, sensitivity training, a variety of simulations, and counseling all are alternatives to the use of role playing. Each has its own particular, unique application.

They reflect the range and variety of strategies and techniques available to the training facilitator who is seriously interested in enriching the learning environment.

WHY ROLE PLAYING?

A human being is complex. Most of us think, feel, and act at the same time. We may not have the three in focus; we may think one thing, say another, and feel a third. The most effective way to reach a person, to communicate with or teach him, is to deal with the totality: the thinking, feeling, behaving individual. It is precisely this that role playing accomplishes. Role playing resembles life more closely than the other training procedures.

A Laboratory Analogy

An analogy can be drawn between a laboratory exercise in biology and the use of role playing to study human problems. In the biology course, the student is provided with a frog and instructed to dissect it, identify the parts, and then draw a picture of it. This method of instruction supplements the student's intellectual understanding of the anatomy of a frog. It provides an opportunity to feel the frog, to become acquainted with the texture and color of its skin, and to cut into the body to explore its internal construction. The laboratory instructor provides guidance on where to cut and how to identify the various parts. Frequently, another specimen is provided so the student can go through the operation again in order to perfect understanding and technique. By the end of the activity, the student not only has a more concrete knowledge of the structure of a frog, but also may have experienced a change in attitude (overcoming of initial distaste, etc.) with an increase in skill and confidence. An important advantage of this type of learning is that the skills can be transferred and generalized to other specimens and activities; they are not restricted in application to the situation within which the original learning took place.

Role playing involves a similar kind of learning. In one type of spontaneous role playing, a situation of personal significance to the participant is identified. The situation involves a human problem between the role player and another person or persons, who usually are not present. Their roles are played by other members of the role-playing group. A typical problem situation is then acted out. Other group members have an opportunity to observe how each role player behaves and to identify the reactions that each member's behavior produces in them. Because it is a training rather than a work situation, group members are free to share their reactions. Suggestions about more effective ways to deal with the problem can be explored; and the situation can be reenacted to test their adequacy.

On the next occasion, role players may exchange roles in order to have the opportunity to explore the situation from the other person's point of view. Again, the action is halted so that each member (or the member who has the actual problem) can describe his or her thoughts and feelings to the others and so they can respond. The action starts again and is repeated until the role player has a more intimate sense of what the real problem is and has had the opportunity to practice alternative ways of dealing with it for use in the real-life situation.

Finally, the problem may be examined from a theoretical and systematic point of view to expand insights regarding the general case, of which the instance under examination is but an example. At this point, however, talking about the problem in more general terms is very different from a lecture because the language is precise and can be related to actual behavior.

In another version of role playing, the people who are actually involved in the problem may be the participants in the kind of laboratory-type analysis just described.

Therapeutic role playing has been used by Peters and Phelan (1957) with industrial supervisors with some success. Additional ways of designing a role-play session are dealt with in later chapters, as are uses of role playing for purposes other than training.

If one has not personally experienced role playing, it might seem that such acting would be superficial and unreal. Quite the opposite is true: it is a common experience that people, when acting out roles, will become emotionally involved, actually begin to behave in a natural manner, and participate intensely and strongly in the situation. This happens even when people had no personal attachment to the role at the beginning. The situation becomes *veridical*—psychologically real.

Role playing is a technique for studying human problems under laboratory-like conditions. The insights and skills thus learned can have a variety of applications far beyond the specific examples practiced, just as laboratory-based learning in the physical or biological sciences generalizes far beyond the specific exercise.

THE BENEFITS OF ROLE PLAYING IN HUMAN RELATIONS TRAINING

There are several distinctive characteristics of the use of role playing as an approach to human relations problems.

Emphasis on Personal Concerns or Problems

Perhaps the most distinguishing feature of role playing is that such training deals with the participants' own concerns. Unlike the study of textbook problems, the analysis of a case, an isolated lecture, or a diagnostic test, the training is tailored to the particular needs of the participant. Impersonal training procedures usually are too abstract, too general, or too focused on problems of the typical or hypothetical person to meet the needs for training, instruction, and evaluation in concrete situations. The importance of dealing with relevant, personal concerns—as emphasized by Bradford (1945)—is difficult to overestimate.

Emphasis on Personal Behavior

An effective learning situation engages a person in actual behavior. How does the person act when confronted with problems that are meaningful and personally significant to him? How could he act differently? If the subject matter being studied is an individual's own behavior, he must accept the learning situation as relevant to his needs. Thus, he is motivated to study, to inquire, and to experiment. He can relate insights obtained to his actual way of behaving in specific situations.

Active Participation

Another positive feature of role playing, as mentioned by Bohart (1977), French (1945), and Moody (1953), is its specific, concrete, *active* approach. Because people act toward one another globally, role playing is able to break through verbal barriers and generate insight and skill where other methods fail. This conclusion is supported in reports by Huyck (1975), Kaull (1954), O'Donnell (1954), and Planty (1948).

In role playing, the artificial separation between thoughts and words on the one hand and action on the other is avoided. The participant has an opportunity to "do," to act in the situation on his own terms. In the traditional classroom situation the student may learn the "right" answers, but gains little or no understanding of them or capacity to apply them. Learning is too likely to be by rote and does not become internalized. Active participation that involves a person in testing his own understanding of a problem and trying new ways of solving it helps to make the learning practical and useful. Role playing provides the individual with the opportunity to participate actively in the subject matter being studied through analyzing, exploring, experimenting, and actually trying out new solutions.

Feedback and Practice

Training to increase social sensitivity, as described by Clore (1971), French (1945), Maier (1953), and Stivers, Buchan, Dettloff, and Orlich (1972), constitutes another use of role playing. Moody (1953) indicates that the method expands social awareness. Frequently, changes in personal attitudes, as mentioned by Stahl (1953), Speroff (1953), and Cohen (1951) result in increased personal respect for the feelings of others. This characteristic of role playing stems from the feedback aspect; it results from participants being provided information about the feelings of others of a kind frequently not discussed in work situations. A person who is more aware of the feeling his behavior evokes in others is able to adjust that behavior more intelligently and in accordance with the impact it produces on others.

When it is possible to "stop the action" here and there for evaluation and to practice alternative modes of reacting, greater possibilities arise for learning about one's behavior.

This time-tested method of helping people learn is used by successful coaches, e.g., in developing tennis players, football teams, golfers, or swimmers. A successful coach may teach out of a book, but he also places the student in the actual situation and provides him with an opportunity to test himself. But the coach does not stop there, either. He works with the person and helps him to identify mistakes. He provides new practice opportunities so that rehearsal of alternative ways of reacting is possible. The model of a coach working with an athlete is much more analogous to role playing in human reactions training than is the model of a teacher lecturing to a group of students, or a father engaged with his son in a "man-to-man" talk.

The use of feedback is essential for instruction based on participation. Other people—often members of the training group—tell an individual how his or her behavior appears to them, or the individual discovers how others were affected by the behavior. Feedback, a basic approach to studying human problems, helps an individual to identify his or her blind spots and to receive the kind of information that one ordinarily fails to see or hear. By checking personal perceptions against those of others, the individual can evaluate his or her own behavior as well as the behavior of others. Alternative ways of behaving that are explored under feedback conditions can be evaluated on the spot. By testing various reactions, one can learn to become more comfortable when acting in new ways.

Role playing also provides an opportunity to practice more skillful ways of relating to others, a value that has been noted by Stahl (1953). The idea of skill practice is as appropriate in improving human relationships as it is in learning any physical skill.

In order to learn about his or her own behavior, a person must feel free to expose personal reactions to examination and evaluation by others. Observers in a role-play situation help the trainee to identify silent assumptions underlying his or her conduct, to assess the impact of the trainee's behavior on others, and to spot behavioral factors that are sources of difficulty. This knowledge can help to increase sensitivity regarding the thoughts and feelings of other people as well as to improve self-understanding and performance. When an opportunity to experiment with and practice alternative ways of behaving is provided, real learning, leading to behavior changes, will occur.

A final feature is that the *method* employed in role playing can be transferred by the participants to analyze new difficulties in *future* situations. Not only do the individuals learn sensitivity and social skills through role playing, they also learn a novel and constructive way to approach the analysis and solution of *any* human problem. This latter aspect has been discussed by Blansfield (1953).

A THEORY OF CHANGE APPLIED TO ROLE PLAYING

No one has yet provided a completely satisfactory theory to explain the value of role playing for the purpose of changing human behavior, although Mead (1934) and Moreno (1953) have explored the subject.

Moreno has defined spontaneity as "an adequate response to a new situation or a new and adequate response to an old situation." The implications are that in any human situation a variety of psychological and interpersonal forces are at work. An individual's ability to react successfully to these forces is dependent on his awareness of them and the freedom with which he can respond once he has become aware. Presumably, we are all inhibited to some extent by our past experience and by a variety of social pressures, which work against free and suitable responses. We might say that people develop established or "frozen" patterns of behavior. Frequently these "historic" patterns are not suitable for dealing with new, immediate problems. Role playing is a device for increasing an individual's ability to deal with the "here and now."

Moreno made a pertinent statement on this subject during a lecture series in 1953; his comments can be paraphrased as follows:

> When a child first begins to become aware of his ability to make sounds he revels in the creative and spontaneous act of experimenting and developing his sound-making facility. He is not concerned with good or bad sounds nor suitable and effective sounds but rather is caught up in the process itself. He soon finds that sounds produce effects and a pattern of sound making begins to develop. He is forced by his parents and society to form sounds into words. Thus, a process which began as an experience in creativity and spontaneity becomes to some extent inhibited and constricted by a variety of pressures and demands. Thus the psychodramatic approach to dealing with functional speech difficulties is to attempt to recreate the spontaneity and creativity in which speech is born. Analogously, role playing in interpersonal relations attempts to create a spontaneous and creative setting in which constricting pressures are removed and the individual has an opportunity to learn in a free and uninhibited way.

Thus, in Moreno's opinion, one of the crucial factors in role playing that leads to behavior change is reduction of inhibitions. Typical inhibitions are fears of criticism, punishment, or ridicule. Since inhibitions prevent spontaneous and creative expression, they must be reduced before changes can occur.

When threats are perceived, an individual is restrained, careful, and conforming. He does not experiment, explore, or try out new modes of acting. To reduce the role player's anxiety, to enable him to invent, play, or experiment with new forms of human interaction, he must "loosen up" or "warm up." The warm-up unlocks an individual, because it frees him from doubts, anxieties, and fears that his new behavior will be criticized, punished, or ridiculed. Role playing has this effect; constricting pressures that prevent consideration and practice of new ways of behaving are removed. Exploration becomes possible. *New* feelings arise, and old feelings are experienced in new contexts. Consequences of new behavior can be evaluated. Practice stabilizes the new behavior, and this stabilization can result in changes being transferred to and practiced in real life.

The type of action that is generally typical of learning through role playing involves starting and halting, moving forward and then falling backward. Lewin's (1958) theory of change explains it as a three-step sequence: (a) unfreezing current patterns of behavior, (b) moving to new behavior patterns, and (c) freezing the new patterns into place.

Unfreezing Current Patterns of Behavior

Commonplace, everyday behavior that an individual executes without thinking is "frozen" behavior. Greeting a visitor, answering the telephone, or conducting a staff meeting in a routine way are examples of frozen behavior, in which little thought about *approach* or *procedure* is required. Full attention can be given to the problem being discussed or the topic being analyzed. Under such conditions, adjustments are so automatic that participants are largely unaware of the procedural foundations of their interaction. As a result, the procedural aspects may be inappropriate, although the individual may not recognize the fact. An example is a person who does not realize that he sounds gruff over the telephone, giving short and curt replies and asking sharp questions. If confronted, the person may say that he "just wanted to cut through to the facts." His way of communicating has become so routine, or frozen, that he cannot hear himself.

Individuals often employ certain automatic assumptions in their approach to any situation. One result is that standard ways of behaving are all that are proposed or tried. An example is in meetings, where certain "givens" are the use of a chairman and recorder, fixed time intervals for discussion, asking for opposing views to be expressed, and the assumption that silence means consent. In role playing, with feedback and an evaluation of what is happening, awareness develops that untested assumptions are being made. This awareness of stereotypical thinking constitutes a first step toward change. Bradford (1945) has emphasized the importance of diagnosing present behavior in supervisory training.

An "unfreezing" period occurs in social learning through role playing. Members become self-consciously aware of their usual approaches and procedural assumptions. Almost every type of behavior generates questions and criticism. Counterproposals are made, and it frequently seems as though no single way of behaving will fit the requirements of the situation.

The period of unfreezing is not comfortable. Anxiety is generated when old styles of behavior are labeled unsatisfactory. The reasons for such tensions are clear, for this represents a period of "unlearning" what already is known but no longer is appropriate. Participants recognize that their own behavior is unsatisfactory, but they have not yet discovered the requirements of more effective action.

Change

This second phase in the learning cycle has three parts, according to Lippitt, Watson, and Westley (1958): developing a clear understanding of the problem; developing several alternative actions that may resolve the problem; and actually trying out one or more of these alternatives. Role playing is useful in all of these subparts of the change phase.

Once there is awareness of a need for changed behavior (unfreezing), the individual must develop this awareness into an understanding and diagnosis of the problem situation. Only then can one create solutions that have a reasonable chance of success. Understanding a problem situation in depth is often facilitated by acting it out. The problem may be specific or general; all the involved parties may or may not be present. These circumstances will have some effect, but regardless of such variations the role-play technique can be used to explore and understand the problem.

Role playing also gives people the opportunity to try out new behaviors in a "safe" setting. One can discover—surprisingly well—how comfortable new behaviors are and which of several alternative actions "fits" best. One can practice and repractice, trying out minor variations repeatedly. Thus, weeks, months, and even years of real-life experience can be simulated in a few role-play sessions. Although the learning may not be quite as powerful as in a real setting, this lack is more than compensated for by the ease, safety, and creative learning potential of the role-play situation.

In role-play settings individuals often receive surprisingly accurate ideas of how others will react to their changed behavior and can, therefore, plan in advance to avoid negative consequence.

Refreezing Behavior Patterns

In this final phase of the learning cycle, role playing can have only peripheral effects, since, according to Lippitt et al. (1958), only the actual practice of new behavior can accomplish the third subpart of the change phase, refreezing. Nonetheless, when the people who are actually involved in the role-play situation are the same ones who interact in real settings, there is a much greater likelihood that changed behavior patterns will be effective and will continue over time. This is due to the change in the expectations of the parties involved. Instead of one person simply showing up one day and exhibiting clearly different behaviors—which may surprise, confuse, or upset the people with whom that person interacts—the group knows why the person's behavior has changed, understands how the change was developed, and in fact participated in the change process. Thus, other group members are likely to support the changed behavior patterns. This kind of social support is crucial for refreezing new patterns of behavior and making the new patterns last.

Even when group members are not present during the role play, the need for social support of new behavior patterns can be defined as a problem, and the role-play technique can be used to work on that issue.

In summary, a series of phases in the learning cycle can be identified: doing the obvious and typical; learning that it does not work and the reasons why; trying other things that also do not work and discovering new ways of behaving that are more effective; and, finally, firmly establishing the new behavior patterns.

There are several ways in which role playing leads to more effective problem solving, in addition to those just reviewed. Anxiety and disturbances about challenging old ways of behaving lessen as participants learn that unfreezing is necessary for change to take place. The period of unfreezing becomes shorter as experience develops. Members learn to learn. With the assistance of effective role-play facilitators (or effective managerial supports) they feel secure about testing a wide range of assumptions, including ones about procedures used in work, in relating to other people, and in searching for alternatives *without* passing through a severe or disturbing phase. Such behavior is properly described as flexible and experimental. Flexible and experimental, ready to test alternatives and to challenge new solutions for old problems is another way of describing a skilled problem solver.

The sequence unfreezing-change-refreezing is a way of describing steps in a process of learning. It has application far beyond role playing. Modern industry, for example, is confronting old, frozen stereotypes regarding products, the way to produce them, and techniques of distribution. New laws require changes in criteria for hiring. In many cases the applications of learning from science or new regulations have not yet been firmly established, so people are unfrozen, dissatisfied with old patterns, but unable to establish new ones. Organizations that are flexible and experimental usually are able to adjust to changing cultural or technical requirements more effectively than organizations that deliberately persist in their traditional ways. The latter frequently do not "wake up" until it is too late.

SUMMARY

In contrast to alternative approaches to understanding and changing behavior, role playing focuses on problems that are of concern to the person. It permits active participation, supported by feedback and practice, with freedom for experimentation of the kind made possible by a "laboratory" setting.

A theory of change based on a three-step cycle of activity from unfreezing behavior to changing behavior patterns to refreezing the new behavior can be used to show that the changes that occur under role-play conditions are unlikely to occur in other approaches to teaching.

REFERENCES

Blake, R. R., & Mouton, J. S. *Making experience work: The grid approach to critique*. New York: McGraw-Hill, 1978.

Blansfield, M. G. Consider "value analysis" to get the most out of role playing. *Personnel Journal*, 1953, *34*, 251-254.

Bohart, A. C. Role playing and interpersonal-conflict reduction. *Journal of Counseling Psychology*, 1977, *24*, 15-24.

Bradford, L. P. Supervisory training as a diagnostic instrument. *Personnel Administration*, 1945, *8*, 3-7.

Clore, G. L., & Jeffery, K. M. *Emotional role playing, attitude change and attraction toward a disabled person*. Paper presented at the Midwestern Psychological Association Convention, Detroit, Michigan, May 6-8, 1971.

Cohen, J. The technique of role-reversal: A preliminary note. *Occupational Psychology*, 1951, *25*, 64-66.

Dooley, A. R., & Skinner, W. Casing casemethod methods. *Academy of Management Review*, April 1977, *2*(2), 277-289.

Forrester, J. W. *World dynamics*. Cambridge, MA: Wright-Allen Press, 1973.

French, J. R. P. Role playing as a method of training foremen. *Sociometry*, 1945, *8*, 410-422.

Huyck, E. T. Teaching for behavioral change. *Humanist Educator*, 1975, *14*, 12-20.

Kaull, J. L. Combining role playing, case study and incident method for human relations training. *Journal of the American Society of Training Directors*, 1954, *8*, 16-19.

Lewin, K. *Field theory in social science*. New York: Harper & Row, 1951.

Lewin, K. Group dynamics and social change. In E. E. Maccoby, T. M. Newcomb, and E. L. Hartley (Eds.), *Readings in social psychology* (3rd ed.). New York: Holt, Rinehart and Winston, 1958.

Lippitt, R., Watson, J., & Westley, B. *The dynamics of planned change*. New York: Harcourt Brace Jovanovich, 1958.

Maier, N. R. F. Dramatized case material as a springboard for role playing. *Group Psychotherapy*, 1953, *6*, 30-42.

Mead, G. H. *Mind, self and society*. Chicago: University of Chicago Press, 1934.

Moody, K. A. Role playing as a training technique. *Journal of Industrial Training*, 1953, 7, 3-5.

Moreno, J. L. Unpublished lecture. New York: The Moreno Institute, 1953.

O'Donnell, W. G. Role playing in training and management development. *Journal of the American Society of Training Directors*, 1954, 8, 76-78.

Peters, G. A., & Phelan, J. G. Practical group psychotherapy reduces supervisor's anxiety. *Personnel Journal*, 1957, 35, 376-378.

Planty, E. G. Training employees and managers. In E. G. Planty, W. S. McCord, & C. A. Efferson (Eds.), *Training employees and managers for production and teamwork*. New York: Ronald Press, 1948.

Schmuck, R. A. Helping teachers improve classroom group processes. In W. W. Charters, N. Gage, & M. Miles, (Eds.), *Readings in the social psychology of education* (2nd ed.). Boston, MA: Allyn & Bacon, 1969.

Speroff, B. J. The group's role in role playing. *Journal of Industrial Training*, 1953, 7, 17-20.

Stahl, G. R. Training directors evaluate role playing. *Journal of Industrial Training*, 1953, 7, 21-29.

Stivers, S. N., Buchan, L. G., Dettloff, C. R., & Orlich, D.C. Humanism: Capstone of an educated person. *Clearing House*, 1972, 46, 556-560.

3

Problems on the Human Side of Organizations

Before planning applications of role playing to training, communication, and evaluation, one needs to consider: what *are* the problems on the *human* side of organizations? This is an important question; if such "people problems" can be identified, ways can be devised to use role playing and other means to help people deal more effectively with these problems.

The typical "people problems" can be classified in five major areas:

1. Power and authority
2. Morale and cohesion
3. Norms and standards
4. Goals and objectives
5. Change and development.

It is in these areas that a range of human difficulties appears within organizational life. A better understanding of the sources of difficulties in each of these areas can help in evaluating how role playing can be used to overcome them.

POWER AND AUTHORITY

The problem of power and authority is a particularly critical source of difficulty in modern society. The general problem has two aspects. First, some persons who *possess* power and authority exercise it ineffectively; others who know they are *subject* to power and authority have trouble accepting that fact, regardless of whether power or authority is presently being exercised upon them and in whatever manner. Second, how people *react* to power and authority can be a factor in increasing or decreasing their effectiveness and personal satisfaction. When attitudes toward authority in general or toward a specific person in authority arouse antagonism or the sense of being threatened, the person who has these feelings becomes less competent to deal objectively with the situation. Thinking may become distorted and self-defeating cycles of behavior may result. This is true whether the authority is an abstract concept such as "The Establishment," or a specific individual such as a boss, a parent, a teacher, or a police officer. When these kinds of difficulties are encountered, the facilitator's task is to use the most appropriate intervention to help people deal with them. Often this intervention will utilize role playing as a central means of change.

Rejection and Suppression

Rejection by someone who is personally significant to oneself and who possesses power or authority—a parent, boss, teacher, or older brother or sister—is certainly a cause of much difficulty. From the standpoint of the person having authority or power, a refusal or put-down given without explanation can quickly eliminate disagreement, re-establish control, and permit "progress" on the authority person's terms. For the person rejected, elimination of disagreement in this way amounts to suppression, pure and simple. The rejected person feels that he has been evaluated and found wanting.

People find rejection and suppression of this sort difficult to take. An immediate reaction is to become antagonistic toward the authority person; often rejected individuals will start fighting back or will respond with bitterness or defensiveness. Others may simply walk out, removing themselves from the authority person's field of power and influence, although in situations of childhood and adult dependency this might be a practical impossibility. Still others, accepting the authority behind the rejection, seem to conclude that they *are* unworthy. They may buckle under and follow commands, but somehow they are not the same from then on.

Whatever the reaction to being rejected through suppression, strong emotions are involved. Feelings such as resentment, hostility, frustration, or self-worthlessness can lead to unhealthy, unproductive, and even self-destructive behavior.

Role playing is ideally suited to aiding people to explore their relationships with people who have different power and authority positions—boss/subordinate, parent/child, doctor/patient, teacher/pupil, minister/parishioner, etc.—and to examine their attitudes toward exercising authority and their reactions to authority exercised by others. The importance of this issue is made obvious by the fact that training in managerial style, or the use of power, has become the most common issue in the field of training and development.

MORALE AND COHESION

Morale and cohesion are used to describe the feeling of esprit de corps, being "in," or feeling a part of things, versus the feeling of being "out," separate or shut off from others.

When a person's feelings of morale and cohesion are high, the person is ready to commit effort. When these feelings are low, commitment is low and the person drags along.

Role playing can be very useful in aiding people who experience low morale to identify what is producing their sense of discouragement or depression, and to practice strategies and alternatives that might help them overcome the discouragement and indecisiveness that result from career problems or from feeling threatened by demotion, the prospect of failure, or loneliness.

Loss of morale and reduced personal cohesion can occur as a result of the loss of a loved one or from the serious challenges to one's self-esteem that arise when one is unable to cope with overwhelming difficulties. Role playing can aid people in such circumstances to experience positive ways of dealing with such difficulties and, in this way, to arrest self-defeating cycles and replace them with positive orientations.

Loss of morale can also result from difficulties in relationships with others. Role playing can be used to aid a husband to identify what in his relationship with his wife is causing him to feel despair and to practice alternative behaviors that can contribute to improving the relationship. In a work-group setting, when an individual feels rejected and does not know why, role playing can be used to investigate what he does that brings rejection and what he may need to learn in order to gain acceptance.

There is much to indicate that lowered morale and cohesion are among the more severe problems confronting contemporary societies. Feelings of alienation, loneliness, and helplessness have become prominent as rural life has been replaced by urban living. It is important that the training facilitator be skilled in using tools to aid people in overcoming such difficulties.

NORMS AND STANDARDS

We know that living together under complex arrangements is possible only because people can interrelate with one another by virtue of sharing. Norms and standards reflect shared expectations that people have of one another. When these expectations are valid, each person can anticipate what the other persons will do and can correlate his or her efforts with others in order to bring about productive outcomes.

There are two aspects of the norms and standards that can be dealt with valuably by the use of role-play techniques. One is that norms and standards, even though informal and never explicitly agreed to, are set at such a low level that they block productive and creative efforts of individuals. People feel the need to adhere to what others are doing, and yet the silent agreement keeps everyone from being as fully productive and occupied as he or she otherwise might be.

The other problem to which role-play techniques can be applied productively involves resistance to change. When norms and standards have been in force for an extended period of time, people accept them as second nature; when efforts are made to change them, resistance is often encountered. The importance of norms and standards is evidenced by the use of terms such as apple polishing, goldbricking, or marking time—phrases that tell us that an individual is either breaking norms and standards by going above or below them or cooperating with norms and standards that are far below what would be appropriate. By exploring attitudes toward silent norms and standards through role playing, it often is possible to aid individuals to see what their silent commitments are and to reject outmoded norms and standards and replace them with shared expectations that are more appropriate to the circumstances.

GOALS AND OBJECTIVES

It is difficult to overestimate the ability of goals and objectives to give character and direction to human endeavors. Goals and objectives offer a meaningful orientation and lend a purpose to any activity. Many activities in modern society are already structured in terms of goals and objectives, e.g., a college education, for which graduation represents the completion of a planned cycle of activity. The goal of business is profit, i.e., planned activities are calculated to increase the return on investment from certain products or reduce the expense of producing or marketing them. Family life and healthy children are the goals of numerous marriages.

Often, however, goals are expressed in such abstract terms or are so remote from activities that behavior is barely influenced. Graduation may be the completion of a college activity cycle, but for the first several years this goal may be too far away to affect conscious endeavor. The same is true of corporate profit. Although certain higher layers in the organization may consider profit crucial, at other levels an individual's contribution to corporate profit is so difficult to evaluate it becomes moot.

The importance of goals and objectives as foundations for meaningful behavior is evident. Role playing can be used in various ways to aid people in (a) clarification of goals, (b) redefinition of goals, (c) restructuring of activities to make goal-oriented actions possible, or (d) setting of goals in situations where it is possible to designate what those goals—especially if unprecedented—should be.

CHANGE AND DEVELOPMENT

A new approach is being used to teach people how to deal with problems; the approach is called *planned change*. On the assumption that if we are unable to change situations we have no choice but to live within the status quo and accept whatever occurs, planned change provides the option to learn the dynamics of change, strategies for causing it, and the skills necessary for bringing about positive change.

This new approach to change differs from older patterns that rely on evolution or one-step-at-a-time processes to bring needed alterations or the use of force and pressure to overwhelm resistance to change.

Neither passive evolution nor the use of force is consistent with the emerging trends of society. Therefore it is critical that training and development facilitators understand the importance of role playing in helping people to change and that they know what the technique entails and how to apply it effectively.

Role playing can be of particular use in exploring attitudes about change because it allows an individual to experience a different kind of behavior and practice doing those things necessary for making a particular change. Indeed, role playing may be one of the best approaches to dealing with resistance to change. Individuals who are confronting a need for change can use role playing to identify their sources of resistance and then explore how to reduce the resistances by finding and practicing alternative strategies of behavior that are required by the change in question; thus, a sense of being able to do things differently or better often results in enthusiasm for change and development, rather than resistance and resentment.

SUMMARY

The range of applications of role playing is very broad; it encompasses such fundamental skills in human effectiveness as (a) identifying uses and misuses of power and authority, (b) identifying and changing situations that cause people to suffer from lowered morale and cohesion, (c) learning how to set appropriate norms and standards, (d) developing skill in setting realistic and attainable goals and objectives, and (e) acquiring an understanding of change and development, sources of resistances to them, and how to resolve the difficulties. These five problem areas are interdependent. When changes are made in any one of them, changes also may be observed in one or more of the others. In general, the group facilitator's effectiveness depends on his or her ability to identify correctly the focal issue and to use role playing flexibly to effect the desired improvement.

TECHNIQUES

4

Preparation for Role Playing

Role playing can be conducted in a wide range of settings; it can be woven into ongoing supervisory training, it can be a major technique in developing interpersonal skills, and it can be used to confront and solve ongoing organizational and interpersonal problems. Obviously, the effectiveness of role playing in any of these settings or applications depends on adequate preparation. There are three major areas in which preparation is essential:

1. The people
2. The situation
3. The facilitator.

The facilitator also must have some knowledge of the group (family, organizational, etc.) milieu, of the norms and standards present in the environment in which participants interact. So the facilitator must be prepared both broadly in terms of knowledge, skill, and application of the technique and specifically in terms of the needs, goals, relationships, and interests of the participants.

PREPARING THE PEOPLE

Whenever a training session is designed and implemented within a group (or organization), the training process is an intervention into the life of that group; that is, it introduces new conditions that affect group members. For example, when industrial supervisors are given special training in how to handle disciplinary problems, complaints, and grievances, the training process itself impacts directly and indirectly on other members of the organization. Employees or union representatives may find themselves dealing with supervisors who are more knowledgeable, skillful, and direct in handling complaints and other difficulties. Top executives and labor-relations specialists may find that the first-line supervisor is taking on more responsibility and behaving differently in the way in which he or she responds to on-the-job problems. Thus, the training process influences and may restructure the way in which people and organizational components interact.

This is particularly true in applying role playing, which, by its nature, brings out feelings and concerns that might not have become visible if didactic training methods had been used. For this reason, both participants in the role-play process and nonparticipants in the organization need to know what to expect.

The Nonparticipants

Members of the organization who will not be participating in the training but who may be directly influenced by its outcomes should have an opportunity to contribute to the definition of objectives and clarification of problems to be dealt with during the training process. This is true, for example, of managers whose subordinates will be participating in the training experience and of family or organizational members who may be affected indirectly by the training endeavor. At the very least, these nonparticipants should be aware of the nature and possible outcomes of the training activity. It is wise for them also to be made aware of the following factors:

1. The sessions are designed—regardless of the specific content—as learning experiences in which people are encouraged to experiment with new behavior. Problem situations may be dealt with out of context; some issues may be magnified for study and experimentation, and there may be some distortion since role plays often are spontaneous and participants improvise as the scenario develops. Therefore, judgments concerning the individual attitudes or organizational behavior of participants should not be made by nonparticipants based on snippets of conversation. (It is advisable for participants to keep the interpersonal and personal actions of their colleagues confidential in order to avoid this kind of misjudgment.)

2. Role playing often involves ventilation of feelings, tensions, and previously unexpressed thoughts and ideas. Many role-play techniques are designed to make it possible for people to "let go" and speak their thoughts; at times this may be risky. On the other hand, it is this very process that makes role playing so impactful and relevant to the real feelings of the people participating. Nonparticipants need to know that trial and error, open and expressive behavior, and spontaneity may result in interactions that may not be typical of what happens on the job but are useful ingredients of the learning process.

The Participants

Participants should be made aware of the same issues that are brought to the attention of nonparticipants: (a) that role playing often is an "opening up" process and (b) that final judgments or decisions should not be based on one or two interactions; rather, the group should continue to grow and explore as it moves more deeply into the content and objectives of the session. Participants also need to know and influence the goals of the session. The process of setting goals incorporates two factors in order for the program to be responsive to the needs of both the participants and the organization.

Participant Involvement. In most instances it is highly desirable to involve participants as early as possible in planning the objectives of the session and in clarifying the methodology. Most participants are aware of their need to learn interpersonal skills. They may suggest problem situations, key issues, and areas for practice and guidance. Participants have data that no one else possesses: they know how they feel, what they want, and the kinds of problems they encounter. Their involvement in clarifying the purposes of the learning process is a sound input into the design and development of the program. This information can be gathered through interviews, questionnaires, or small-group discussions.

Organization-Based Data. To identify specific organizational needs and goals regarding the session being planned, top managers may be asked to identify program objectives. Training committees, personnel and training specialists, or outside consultants also may identify needs for additional or specialized training. These needs and goals may be identified through the use of written surveys.

In most organizations there are hard criteria for examining organizational effectiveness; e.g., hospitals have data regarding patient care and health-service procedures, and public schools have ways to measure teacher performance and student and parent attitudes. In every organization there are bottom-line expectations or goals; data concerning how performance meets these goals can be used to ascertain training needs and objectives.

In summary, the facilitator should communicate to others what role playing is and what it can do and should learn as much as possible about the nature of the milieu in which the process will take place. During the training process, the facilitator must create a climate of relative freedom and acceptance within the group so that if an equivocal situation arises, a favorable attitude can be sustained.

PREPARING THE ROLE-PLAY DESIGN

When all preparatory steps have been taken, the facilitator must prepare the situation. This involves both physical preparation and the preparation of a role-play or training design.

There are two basic design frameworks for a role-play experience: (a) the structured design and (b) the unstructured design, or developmental role play. In order to clarify these two design strategies it is necessary to define "structure"; it refers to the set of relationships that exist among interdependent elements of a given system. For example, an organizational chart illustrates structure by picturing the set of relationships, based on their authority and responsibility, that exists among organizational members. Similarly, the term *sentence structure* refers to the relationships of the key elements, i.e., subject, verb, direct object, in a given set of words. All role-play situations have structure. There are sets of relationships between role-playing participants (boss-subordinate, friend-foe, engineer-accountant, etc.). There are also situational factors that become part of the structure of the role play. Identification of circumstances such as increasing costs, organizational members who resist new policies, or strong interdepartmental competition can assist trainees in understanding the nature of the structure in which the situation is occurring and the dynamics or processes that are taking place within that structure. In any role-play experience, individuals are either given or gradually develop knowledge of the relationships among key participants in the role play as well as other critical relationships that affect organizational behavior, performance, finances, the quality of services, and so on.

Structured Role-Play Designs

A role play is designated as structured when the facilitator (or others involved in the design of the session) determines the structure and makes it explicit to participants. Participants are provided with instructions that point out the relationships between key characters in the role play and often include a background sheet that delineates important characteristics, situations, and other relevant information. Structured role plays often include an explicit statement of the goals and issues that will be confronted both by those participating actively in the role play and those involved as observers.

Basically, then, in a structured role play, the designers have predetermined the goals of the session and the critical relationships with which the session has been designed to cope. There is still ample room for participants to experiment with new behavior, try out a variety of techniques, and determine various courses of action that they feel are important. However, in a structured role play the group is responding to situations, issues, and materials provided by the facilitator. These issues will have been developed from a careful examination of the trainees' interests and needs. Materials may be changed on the spot or in follow-up sessions in order to more clearly pinpoint critical problems. Nevertheless, the structure is largely preplanned, rather than evolved from spontaneous interests. There are preparatory ground rules to be used in designing a structured role play:

1. A *specific purpose and set of behavioral objectives* should be defined through the use of surveys, interviews, analyses of current data, or a more generalized analysis of training needs.
2. *Critical problems and goals* that relate to these objectives should be identified prior to the session and should influence the design of materials, instruments, and role-play processes.
3. *Instructions* for role players, observers, and other participants should be prepared and tested in advance.
4. A *format* to induce appropriate discussion of key issues should be part of the role-play design.

A brief example of a set of role-play materials is presented here. The objectives and instructions also are included, since these materials are designed to be used by the facilitator. The example is condensed.

HANDLING DISAGREEMENT THROUGH EFFECTIVE LISTENING

Goal (stated to the group)

To increase the ability of supervisors and managers to listen effectively when confronted with disagreement or resistance.

Specific Behavioral Objectives (for the facilitator)

1. Participants will increase their skill in using questions, general statements, paraphrasing, and other nondirective or active-listening responses, specifically when confronted with feelings or ideas with which they may disagree.
2. Supervisors will increase their capacity to give and receive feedback without defensiveness.

Instructions (for the facilitator)

1. After a brief discussion of the purpose of the session, each participant is given a brief role and background information sheet. The group is then divided into teams of three members each.
2. One member of each subgroup is designated as member A, another as member B, and the third as the observer. Each member is given a sheet of instructions pertinent to his or her role.

Role Instructions (Member A)

Your role during the first phase of this activity is to listen and ask questions without pursuing your own opinion or attempting to force the other person into a conclusion that agrees with your own. You may, from time to time, state ideas; however, you are not to attempt to change the other person's point of view. Your goal is to listen and understand. The following information is provided to guide you in this effort.

Appropriate Listening Responses:

1. General questions (What do you think? What happened?) are useful in finding out more about what another person thinks. Loaded questions or questions that lead to a predetermined answer (Don't you think you should be more reasonable?) are inappropriate.
2. Statements that encourage the person to talk (Tell me more about it; I'm interested in some of your other feelings) tend to increase communication.
3. Paraphrasing or nondirective responses (sometimes called active-listening responses) that pick up what the other person has said and feed it back may be useful. For example, if a person says, "I think women are becoming too aggressive and belligerent in trying to get ahead," the interviewer might say, "I see, you think that women are abrasive in the way in which they are pursuing their goals." This kind of response encourages the other person to talk.

Your partner (role player B) will initiate the discussion.

Role Instructions (Member B)

During the role-play situation you are to express your opinions freely. If you encounter resistance or disagreement you may deal with it any way you see fit. You are asked not to play a part but to express your genuine feelings about the issue and pursue your point of view in order to clarify the issue, influence the other person's opinion, or simply get your own position stated. You are to initiate the discussion by introducing your point of view about this statement: *Women are treated unfairly in most organizations. Males dominate the scene and often are unaware of their chauvinistic behavior.*

Observer Guide

During the course of the role-play discussion, observe Member A. Did he or she (check statements that apply):

——Quickly reveal his or her own point of view and push for a favorite point?
——Ask questions that suggest a desired answer (leading or loaded questions)?
——Seem interested in drawing out and understanding the viewpoint of the other?
——Occasionally paraphrase what the other person said or use other nondirective techniques to draw out additional information?

Comment on ways in which the interviewer kept the discussion going:

Summary (for the facilitator)

Conduct a brief discussion of the role-play activity, drawing out observers and participants in order to clarify the nature of the listening process and ways in which diverse viewpoints can be pursued. Discussion items include:

1. Which responses by the supervisor seemed to encourage the interviewee to talk more?
2. What comments seemed to discourage the interviewee or put him or her on the defensive?
3. Were the observers or member B quickly able to discern the interviewer's motives and goals or did the interviewer maintain an open listening posture?
4. Construct a list of the kinds of comments, approaches, and attitudes that seem to improve the quality of listening.

Note: This brief, structured role play can be used to introduce the subject of listening skills. It has been *condensed* to illustrate key elements in the design of a structured role play. For more sources of structured role plays, see the Appendix; Maier, Solem, and Maier (1975); and Pfeiffer and Jones (1969-1979).

Unstructured or Developmental Role-Play Designs

In unstructured role-play situations, the relationships between key role players or various elements of the situation are developed with and by group members. Participants are not supplied with detailed instructions, written role instructions, observer guides, notes, etc. The role-play facilitator engages people in defining critical elements of the situation and in developing interactions or role plays that will help to explore and expand on those situations.

Thus, in a developmental role-play session the structure emerges from the group—based on members' relationships, interests, and concerns—rather than from a situation predesigned by the facilitator. However, in an unstructured session the facilitator may use observer guides, audio or videotape replay, and other techniques and methods in order to enhance the learning process. Essentially, the critical ground rule for conducting unstructured sessions is to avoid imposing relationships, orientations, or evaluative data on the group. Processes for developing an appropriate climate and facilitating the emergence of key issues and relationships will be described in Chapter 5.

PREPARING THE PHYSICAL SETTING

Much of the success of role playing depends on the physical location and surroundings in which it takes place.

Location

The ideal location has three characteristics:

Proper Size. The room should have a minimum of twenty-five to a maximum of fifty square feet per participant. Very small or very large rooms are not suitable. If one has to make a choice between two unsuitable locations, a smaller room is generally preferred.

Privacy. The role-play location should have no distractions. No outside person should enter the room or be able to look into it or be able to overhear what is going on. Participants should not be interrupted by telephone calls or visitors. The room should be quiet, and extraneous noises, such as outside voices, should be avoided.

Flexibility. The room should not have fixed furniture. A classroom or an auditorium with fixed seats is an example of a poor location.

It frequently is difficult to obtain a proper location; the ingenious facilitator will requisition a suitable executive office if no better location is available.

Scheduling

It is a challenge to arrange a schedule that is not irksome to at least some of the participants. Furthermore, a schedule that is convenient for the individuals may be inconvenient for the organization. Compromises may well have to be made; but unless the time selected can contribute to effective learning, the facilitator should confront the issues that are blocking appropriate arrangements.

Arrangements

The general rule for placement of furniture is that there should be no pieces in the room beyond those needed and that items should be arranged to permit maximum visual and verbal communication between all members. A long conference room with a narrow table is an example of a particularly poor arrangement.

Extra pieces of furniture should be removed from the room if possible. If not, they should be grouped in a corner out of the way and, if possible, separated from the rest of the room by screens. Chairs and tables to be used should be neatly arranged so that individuals can go to their proper places without difficulty.

PREPARING THE FACILITATOR

Role playing is a technique, similar to the interview; with a little instruction any person capable of conducting an effective interview can learn to conduct a role play. Most role-play facilitators probably are similar in their personalities, abilities, or backgrounds to other training facilitators. However, we can make some generalizations about the important qualifications, personal and technical, of effective role-play facilitators.

Personality

The good facilitator is an "open" rather than a "closed" type of person and should be friendly and flexible. A good sense of orientation—which means that the trainer can see the trees *and* the forest in any problem—is highly desirable. The facilitator must know what is going on and have a keen sense of awareness of the relative importance of situations. He or she must be adroit, i.e., have the tact and sensitivity to deal with people and the capacity to straighten out complexities and entanglements. Persuasiveness and the capacity to get people to understand what is going on and to want to participate is critical. The facilitator must have good judgment and be able to assess situations and make rapid decisions of good quality. Beyond all this, the really good facilitator is sincere. His or her openness and concern for the feelings and rights of group members are functions of a personal belief system, not a pose. This combination of qualities will give individuals confidence in the facilitator and will facilitate the movement desired. The personality of the facilitator is of far greater importance than his or her technical qualifications.

Training

At the present time we have no reliable information regarding the necessary background training needed by a role-play facilitator. There are no data to show that a person trained in the social sciences is more effective than one trained in the biological or physical sciences, that a psychologist is any better than a teacher, or a teacher any better than someone else. It would appear, everything else being constant, that the best prepared individuals are those who have a good background in the behavioral sciences, specifically in human relations areas. However, some individuals who are poorly prepared academically are sometimes found to be "naturals" for role playing and can be more effective than people with excellent academic backgrounds.

If it is kept in mind that role playing may have many levels of competence, and that for some levels high degrees of ability are not necessary, even poorly trained and poorly qualified people can do satisfactory jobs when not too much skill is called for. No matter how poorly prepared a facilitator may be, he can improve his understanding and capacity by proper preparation—through reading and study, but most of all by observation and participation in other role-playing groups. The conscientious facilitator will take advantage of courses and seminars given in this area by universities, private consulting firms, and professional societies.

Functions

The role-play facilitator need not be an expert in the participants' field of specialization. A *facilitator* is not a *teacher*. (The writers of this book have done role playing with teachers, nurses, prison guards, army officers, salespeople, business executives, and training directors.)

If the facilitator should happen to have technical knowledge of the field in which the participants are interested, he or she may wish to suppress this information so as not to confuse the role of facilitator with that of expert. The facilitator may wish to become a resource person who may inject opinions with reference to proper role behavior, but it is usually wise not to try to play the role of both facilitator and expert.

Assistants

In most cases the facilitator works alone. However, assistants who do not attend group sessions primarily for their own benefit but rather to assist the facilitator can be helpful.

Protagonists. The primary person in a role-play session is called the protagonist, the one who is to be trained or evaluated. The protagonist interacts with other individuals, called assistants or antagonists, who may take a variety of roles. Antagonists generally come from the group, sometimes being selected by the protagonist, sometimes by volunteers, and sometimes being assigned by the facilitator.

A trained assistant is frequently useful, especially when role playing is done for information giving or for evaluation. The trained assistant operates in a more uniform manner than one who is not trained, and so provides a more constant stimulus to the protagonist. Trained assistants are especially valuable in the "doubling" technique (see Chapter 6) since they are sensitized to how people think. In using complicated techniques or when multiple groups are employed, trained assistants can be invaluable in reducing confusion.

Observers. Frequently, the facilitator may wish to use assistants as nonparticipating observers who will report back to the group their observations and conclusions. While some members of any group can be given these roles, trained observers— especially those who have observed similar situations in other groups—can be helpful. Not being personally involved in the training situation or with the individuals, these assistants provide expert objective summaries and evaluations. If somewhat complicated observer guides are used, the assistants can employ them properly. When a group of trained observers have a general understanding of the facilitator's purposes, they can assist the group in its development.

SUMMARY

Perfection depends on trifles, but perfection is not a trifle. Successful role playing depends on many interlocking and interacting elements and demands adequate preparation. One element out of kilter—a microphone that does not work, the loss of case material, or misunderstandings by one or more members—can throw a session out of functional commission. The facilitator must plan his or her sessions well. Effectiveness depends to a great extent on a natural, easy, and spontaneous approach, which frequently calls for considerable prior work. What the facilitator does during a session represents only a small fraction of what is done overall.

REFERENCES

Maier, N. R. F., Solem, A. R., & Maier, A. A. *The role-play technique: A handbook for management and leadership practice.* San Diego, CA: University Associates, 1975.

Pfeiffer, J. W., & Jones, J. E. *A handbook of structured experiences for human relations training* (7 vols.). San Diego, CA: University Associates, 1969-1979.

5

The Role-Play Process

A number of people have identified various phases in role playing. Shaw suggests three: (a) warm-up, (b) enactment, and (c) post-session analysis. In an anonymously written article (1949), five phases are suggested: (a) establish principles, (b) brief on problems, (c) act out, (d) make recordings, and (e) have discussions. Liveright (1951) lists six divisions: (a) choose problem, (b) agree on details, (c) define roles, (d) instruct observers, (e) act out, and (f) discuss. Bavelas (1947) suggests no fewer than 14 steps, which the reader will find summarized in the Annotated Bibliography.

In this chapter a four-step sequence will be used to identify the key phases in the role-play process:

1. Climate setting: The development of an open, action-oriented climate in the group must take place before meaningful involvement and learning can occur. Climate setting involves orienting the group members regarding the topic: facts, principles, background, etc. It also involves warming up the group, encouraging emotional involvement, and facilitating interaction.

2. Action: Interactions between group members through role playing is the core of the process.

3. Feedback: Post-enactment discussions and analyses of role-playing interactions facilitate learning and prepare people for new action.

4. Generalizing: By extracting general principles and summarizing key skills, the facilitator integrates the learning experience.

In discussing each of these key phases a distinction will be made between structured and unstructured, or developmental, role plays. In preplanned and predesigned sessions in which goals, relationships, and content have been carefully prepared in advance, the phases of the process are handled somewhat differently than when the structure of the role play emerges from group discussion and ongoing interactions.

CLIMATE SETTING

Structured Role Playing

Orienting the group requires substantive input and discussion to specify and clarify the problems and goals relevant to the topic. Warming up the group involves preparing members emotionally to take part in a role-play enactment. In a structured session these steps are accomplished by careful design of materials. As indicated in Chapter 4, the facilitator's role-play design is based on an assessment of needs and program and session goals. It includes a definition of objectives and is aimed at engaging people in pursuing objectives—these may include the acquisition of knowledge or skill and the development of more affirmative attitudes and feelings regarding the topic situation.

Two basic procedures are employed in structured role-play sessions. First, the session may be conducted with small groups operating simultaneously. This is referred to as *multiple-group role playing*. The typical setup for multiple role playing is to divide the total group into teams of two or more people. Each team is assigned a task and role-play activity. Each team then interacts independently. One or more team members often serve as observers, and feedback is given. In most multiple role plays, the teams reconvene in a general session to compare and share their experiences and to extract broad principles from the process. Alternatively, the design may focus on two individuals (or small groups), with the rest of the participants serving as an audience or as observers. This is known as *single-group role playing*.

The orientation or climate-setting procedure in either case is facilitated by a wide range of introductory activities. The session may begin with a simple statement of purpose: "We are here today to talk about handling sales objections, and we will begin to work on this issue by examining some typical problem situations." Or "As you know, many patients (or clients) have been complaining about the quality of service that we have been providing. We will review some typical patient complaints by asking all of you to become engaged in handling some patient-care problems." The facilitator may then conduct additional warm-up activities such as engaging the group in a discussion of key issues or may direct several people in an enactment to begin to explore the problem under discussion.

More elaborate orientation and warm-up processes can be used, including lectures, videotapes, or case studies that begin to define key issues and focus the group's attention on problems that will be addressed in the role-play enactments. For example, a film on appropriate techniques for performance review may be presented. The group may then be encouraged to discuss the principles presented and to examine the quality of the interaction portrayed on the screen. Based on this discussion, the group members become more aware of basic principles, techniques, and problems encountered in performance review; they therefore are more ready to begin to practice new skills or to re-examine past performance-review systems and procedures.

Regardless of the specific media or devices used to introduce and clarify key issues, the most important component of the warm-up and orientation process is the discussion that follows and is based on the initial presentation. The following are a few examples of warm-up techniques that can be used in preparation for conducting a structured role play.

Example 1: Performance Management. In a program for managers concerned with reviewing and improving the performance of their subordinates, the purpose of the warm-up process would be to engage all group members in a discussion of their own experiences on the receiving end of performance reviews. Typical discussion questions include: "How do you usually feel when you sit down with a manager who is about to review your performance?" "What has happened in your past experience that made it easy for you to respond when your performance was being criticized or analyzed?" "What do you think are the most important and desirable components to have present when you are engaged by your boss in a discussion of your own performance?"

A list can be prepared on a newsprint pad or chalkboard to summarize key feelings and goals such as: "I believe that the process works best when I am convinced that the boss is trying to undersand how I have been performing, rather than simply evaluating me." "I know that I am uncomfortable when I am sure the boss has already made up his mind and it is not really a discussion but simply an evaluation." These and similar comments begin to set up a framework for conducting prepared role-play enactments. The facilitator then would assign specific roles and observer formats that build on the warm-up discussion. For example, the facilitator might say, "We have listed the key issues that we feel are important during a performance review. In the role-play case that you are about to experience, one member of your group will be asked to serve as an observer. He or she can comment on the degree to which the conditions we have outlined have been met." Thus, the group itself will have, in effect, designed the observer guide or supplemented an existing observer guide as a result of the warm-up discussion.

Example 2: Handling Customer Complaints. A similar form of warm-up occurs when the facilitator presents a procedure or set of conditions to be met in the role-play enactment. For example, the facilitator may outline a procedure for handling customer complaints, such as (a) listen to the customer, (b) get details on the complaint, (c) indicate policy while remaining polite and helpful, (d) suggest a course of action. Some group members would then be asked to take the role of the complaining customer while others take the normal organizational role. Roles may be written in advance to cover typical customer concerns. Multiple role playing, in which the members move from the discussion of the procedure into a practice session with observers, can be used. Alternatively, several people can be asked to try out the procedure in a demonstration role play with the audience divided into observer teams. A typical observer format would be to ask half the group to observe the complaining customer and subsequently feed back what they perceived to be his feelings, attitudes, and major concerns. The second half of the group would observe the member who is handling the complaint and would be asked to make note of this person's feelings, attitudes, and concerns during the role play.

A Word of Caution: When one has asked people to role play a problem in front of a group, it is extremely important to ensure that the process does not become highly critical or evaluative. Many people are discouraged from participation in role-play enactments if their past experience has shown them that the role play is used as a basis for criticizing and analyzing performance. When observers are asked to criticize one of their fellows, they often get "carried away" and end up making the role players feel incompetent, defensive, and angry. The best way to handle a warm-up for a group in which there is to be a role-play demonstration in front of the room is to emphasize that the goal is not to evaluate or criticize role players but rather to experiment with new behaviors, to become more aware of the feelings and concerns of others, and to establish a climate in which people feel free to become spontaneous.

Critical or negative feedback is much easier to handle in multiple role playing. First, there is a small group, usually with one observer, so the impact of the feedback is not as general, as visible, or as embarrassing to individual role players. In multiple role plays there is a chance for all members of the small group to try out new behavior, and all members often have a chance to be observers. The individual does not feel singled out for evaluation and criticism. In small-group settings there is a great deal of opportunity for people to try several approaches, rather than to feel the pressure of being observed by a large group and expected to "perform."

The best precaution against overly critical and embarrassing feedback sessions is to design the feedback process so that it creates awareness and sensitivity rather than becomes a vehicle for criticism or evaluation. A basic approach is to ask for affirmative feedback: "What are some of the things the manager did that you thought were particularly effective?" "In what ways did the counselor indicate his or her concern and awareness regarding the other person's feelings and points of view?" A somewhat different approach is to focus on the procedure rather than the person. The facilitator might say, "We spoke earlier of a four-step procedure for handling customer complaints. Which of these steps did you see demonstrated during the last role play?" Or, "Which steps do you feel might have been extended or used to greater advantage during the session?"

Regardless of specific techniques utilized during the process of acclimating participants to the issues involved and preparing them for involvement, it is important to establish a climate of openness and spontaneity, a non-evaluative, nonpunitive climate in which experimentation and free exchange of information will occur.

Unstructured/Developmental Role Playing

In orienting and warming up a group for an unstructured role play, the emphasis of the process is on the group itself. There is usually a limited amount of input. The group identifies issues and concerns. Typically, a general area of concern or purpose of the session has been designated by the facilitator, e.g., "Handling Employee Complaints" or "Improving the Quality of Vocational Guidance" or "Developing Skills in Resolving Conflict." Given a general area of concern, the facilitator then conducts a warm-up session, usually by beginning with a problem census. Typical problem-census questions are: (a) What are some of the major issues you have confronted in trying to get employees to be more responsive to discussions of their performance? (b) What are the major problems you have encountered in trying to resolve conflicts with other managers?

In unstructured role playing the warm-up is an essential determinant of the effectiveness of the enactment that follows. If the facilitator selects the first problem that comes to the surface without testing for common concerns about that problem, the focus of the session may be on an issue that is of interest to a very small number of people. For example, in a discussion of counseling problems one member of the group might say, "The major problem I have encountered is with young people who have their minds made up about what they want to do and are unwilling to examine their own potential." If the facilitator selects that as the key problem, puts a great deal of energy into working it through, and then learns that very few group members feel that this is a critical or common problem, a great deal of group time and energy will have been wasted. Whenever an issue is raised it is desirable for the facilitator to ask, "Is that issue one that others of you have run into?" "All right, that is one problem that group members have encountered; what other problems have you been aware of?"

Gradually, as questions and issues are surfaced, the facilitator can begin to test for the degree of concern regarding them by saying, "Is this a problem that most of you have encountred? Let's talk about it a little." In some cases the facilitator may simply ask for a vote or show of hands to indicate the relevance of the problem. In any case, the warm-up continues until the facilitator and the group members feel that a key issue has been isolated and that it is worth working on.

Finally, an orientation and warm-up for a developmental session need not be limited to spontaneous group discussion. All the techniques used in structured role playing (films, videotapes, printed materials, case studies, simulations, etc.) can be used to stimulate group concern about a given issue or problem. The distinguishing characteristic of an unstructured role play is that the facilitator (or the material designed by the training staff) does not predetermine the relationships or the processes that take place when the enactment begins. Written role descriptions, background sheets, and predetermined problems are not used. Very often, in unstructured sessions, participants deal with their own unique concerns and relationships while at the same time working on problems of general concern.

Thus, the general concern in a given session might be "how to deal with authoritarian doctors." A specific group member (nurse, administrator, or paramedical person) might then use a real situation involving a real doctor as the specific focus for the enactment.

ACTION

The nature of the role-play enactment is influenced by the nature and amount of structure provided. As indicated earlier, when predetermined goals have been established, and when relationships are defined in advance of the session and set forth in various role descriptions, the session is thought of as a structured role play. When problems and issues emerge from the group—even though a general theme or objective has been identified—and when there are no prescribed relationships or detailed background provided, the session is a developmental role play. The enactment process and the role of the facilitator in a structured session are significantly different from the nature of the process and the facilitator's role in an unstructured session.

Structured Role Playing

In most structured role-play situations the nature of the enactment is in large measure dictated by the design of the role-play procedure. The facilitator makes few interventions because background sheets, role descriptions, observer guides, and other sets of instructions are the major energizing factors in the situation; the interventions have been predesigned into the materials being used. As described earlier, the facilitator identifies purposes prior to the session and determines behavioral objectives as part of the design process. Situational descriptions and roles are written in order to evoke learning opportunities relevant to these predetermined goals and objectives. Within the framework of the structured role play there is a wide range of options and designs available, ranging from very brief role descriptions with limited background information to highly detailed sets of instructions, conditions, and role descriptions. Samples of relatively simple structured role-play situations as well as more complex and detailed designs are found in Appendix 1. Regardless of the specific nature of the role play and the degree to which it is detailed, the enactment process in a structured session is comprised of three steps.

Step 1: Provide Background and Assign Roles. After an appropriate warm-up or orientation, two or more individuals are chosen to enact the role-play scene or situation. They are provided with written or oral instructions regarding their roles. In multiple role-play sessions small groups are formed and pairs or trios of people enact the role play simultaneously. Often members simply are asked to form small groups in various parts of the room, although in prolonged sessions separate rooms may be set aside for detailed role-play involvements. Appropriate background information, usually in written form, is provided.

Step 2: Provide for Interventions. In most structured sessions, interventions are built into the role-play process. They may take a variety of forms:

1. Intervention Through Observers: One or more people may be assigned various observer functions during a role play. In multiple role playing it is typical, for example, to have two persons enact a manager and subordinate, a sales representative and customer, or a counselor and counselee and to have one or more persons observe the interaction with prepared formats for feedback and with sheets for note taking. The observer guide or feedback sheet is structured to highlight predetermined issues and goals that are built into the session. For example, if the focus of a given session is on interviewing skills, various interviewing techniques would be identified on the observer's guide. Key principles or skills to be observed are presented during Step 1 in lecture or demonstration form, and observers feed back "performance" against these guidelines as a basis for improvement among the players.

2. Intervention Through Role Rotation: In order to expose various dimensions of the problem and to contrast various techniques and styles, individual role players may be asked to rotate or reverse roles. In a demonstration or "front-of-the-room" role play the key player (protagonist) may be asked to take on the role of the supporting player based on his or her understanding of that role as it was portrayed in the previous enactment. In multiple role playing, it is often useful to have members of the role-playing team rotate positions; i.e., in a managerial situation the manager becomes the subordinate, the subordinate becomes the observer, and the observer becomes the manager.

3. Intervention Through Feedback from Participants: Participants in the role play may themselves be asked to fill out reaction sheets after the role play has concluded. For example, the person practicing the role of counselor may be given a sheet designed to identify major areas of resistance and the degree to which the "counselor" felt that empathy was established. Simultaneously, the person playing the role of counselee might be asked to answer similar questions. Thus, by exchanging views after an enactment, the participants themselves may become more aware of differences in perception, gaps in understanding, and opportunities for "tuning in" in interpersonal situations.

4. Intervention Through Information: At the close of an enactment, participants may be provided with comparative solutions to the issue they have been working on. For example, in a multiple role-play situation in which trios are asked to play the roles of foreman, shop steward, and employee, the role players may be asked to develop a course of action based on their

discussion. Comparative courses of action or solutions then may be distributed to members so that they can contrast their results with the results of other groups, with "ideal" solutions, or with solutions that are compatible with a union contract. It is important to note that when "ideal" or comparative solutions are prescribed, players who have invested energy and thought into developing a solution to which they are committed may become defensive. For the most part, contrasting solutions should be introduced early in the process so that members have a chance to integrate these solutions into their own plans and try out new behavior rather than simply receiving an evaluation after the fact.

Step 3: A Second Enactment. It is highly desirable after an intervention has been made to provide opportunities for participants to learn from that intervention, to try out new techniques and new approaches. Some interventions are merely replays of the earlier enactment, i.e., people are asked to rotate roles or to switch positions. When a "front-of-the-room" role play is being conducted, other members of the group may be asked to join the role play. In other instances, new input can be provided through lecture materials, films, or other informational sources so that the participants can role play more complex situations or experiment with more sophisticated techniques.

In many role plays the situation itself is structured to provide enactments, interventions, and new enactments. For example, in computer simulations or business games, participants take on various roles (president, financial officer, production manager, etc.), begin to work on a series of problems, and then receive feedback regarding their effectiveness. During these feedback sessions many of the techniques outlined previously can be utilized. For example, observers can be used to give feedback, or individuals within the group can fill out response or reaction sheets that become the basis for analyzing and learning from the enactments.

Business games usually are played in terms of fiscal quarters; that is, participants make a series of business decisions representing business operations for a three-month period. These decisions are programed into a computer that feeds back the business effect of the decisions. The team then pauses for analysis, feedback, and planning. The members then move back into the enactment to make a new series of business decisions. Each enactment provides an opportunity for experimenting with new techniques, utilizing and applying new information, and learning from the insights and feedback provided by others.

In specialized techniques such as behavior rehearsal and behavior modeling (see Chapter 10), interventions are structured into the role-play process. For example, participants try out a given set of roles, receive feedback on their performances, and then try the roles again. Alternatively, participants may react to one carefully designed situation by role playing that situation and then receiving feedback on their effectiveness. Then they may be provided with a second situation and additional feedback is based on the second enactment.

In summary, structured role playing is facilitated by the design itself, by the instruments, materials, and guidelines that are provided by the designer. The facilitator rarely intervenes and, for the most part, such interventions are procedural. Maier, Solem, and Maier (1975) outline the purpose of the structured role play by pointing out that group members move from a discussion of general principles to engagement in a specific issue to generalization from those principles to derivation of applications and on to the identification and practice of new behaviors.

It is always true that when persons participate in the give-and-take that is characteristic of a role play there are innumerable opportunities for increasing self-awareness, sensitivity, skill, and knowledge *without* overt or direct feedback or analysis. Structured role playing, however, is designed to ensure that key issues will be raised through the design itself and that feedback and analysis will focus on issues that are important in order to achieve desired objectives. For example, in a session designed to increase employment interviewers' knowledge of and skill in adhering to legal requirements prescribed in guidelines from the Equal Employment Opportunities Commission, it is not enough to simply hope that appropriate interactions and learning will occur. Role-play incidents must be designed to surface critical issues, and observer guides and feedback sheets must be designed similarly to ensure that these issues are discussed, analyzed, and appropriately resolved.

Unstructured/Developmental Role Playing

In developmental sessions the major source of interventions is the facilitator, who may intervene by guiding the way in which issues or situations are structured, by encouraging group discussion or feedback, or by using a wide range of techniques that will be described in a later chapter. Developmental role-play enactments are therefore highly dependent on the creativity and skill of the facilitator and on the way in which the process is managed. How are the problems identified? How are people moved in and out of key problems in ways that are useful and constructive? How is role flexibility, spontaneity, and creative interaction enhanced? How is the enactment used to generate deeper understanding and to improve self-awareness and skill? The answers to these questions lie in the process and techniques by which the facilitator involves the participants and enables them to move toward experimentation with new behavior and the development of new awareness.

Facilitating a Developmental Role Play

Develop Group Consensus Around a Key Issue. The role-play facilitator may prescribe a general theme or objective for the session but, in a developmental or unstructured process, cannot prescribe the content of the interactions. Nor can the specific situation to be dealt with be imposed upon the group. Therefore, it is critical for the facilitator to spend whatever time is needed to engage the group members in connecting with each other's concerns and problems and becoming aware of a group focus rather than an individual focus.

For example, in working with a group of public school teachers it became apparent that quite a few individuals were concerned with their ability to handle student counseling situations when the student was resentful or hostile. Others felt that the key issue in student counseling was the teacher's capacity to avoid imposing his or her views on the students. Still others were concerned about students who seemed unwilling to make commitments. Clearly, any one of these situations could have become the focus for the role play. It is essential, however, for the facilitator to draw out a problem issue that is shared by all members. Common links must be established so that all group members feel some degree of ownership of the problem that is to be worked on. The first issue in facilitating the enactment, therefore, is to ensure that the group is focusing on an area of common concern or to shift areas of concern until one is identified that is meaningful and engaging for all participants.

One of the most common concerns of those beginning to apply role-play techniques in unstructured situations is the problem of obtaining responsive participants. These are numerous ways in which people can be encouraged to join the enactment comfortably and spontaneously.

Ask for Volunteers. Often there are group members who are eager to try out new behavior or to experiment with new techniques. Other group members may want to test their current modes of handling critical situations. Still others may enjoy the chance to do a little "acting." To encourage these people, the facilitator may say, "We have talked quite a bit about some of the problems in vocational counseling. It would be useful to all of us if someone in the group would show us some of the ways in which he or she deals with resistance from a student. First let us define some of the kinds of resistance we encounter, and that will move us closer to selecting a problem situation." Often group members will begin to describe issues relevant to the topic and thereby will tend to nominate themselves for involvement. A group member may say, "I have one student with whom I think I have tried everything. I have tried to sell him on trying new things, I have been nondirective, I have even gotten angry a few times, but nothing seems to move him." After some additional exploration the facilitator may ask this individual to demonstrate some of the ways in which he or she has responded to the student so that other group members can begin to identify the variety of techniques that are available.

Make the Situation Nonevaluative. The way in which the facilitator leads the discussion will indicate whether or not the focus of the process is on evaluation. A statement such as "Let's see how well people handle this kind of problem" is apt to discourage participation. Compare it with a statement such as "There are probably dozens of ways of responding to this kind of issue. It would be helpful to all of us to take a look at three or four different ways of handling the problem and perhaps then to begin experimenting with new approaches in order to broaden the range of alternatives available to us." Often the facilitator can make a wide-ranging statement to establish the idea that the role-play process is experimental rather than evaluative: "One of our purposes today is to try handling problems in new ways. We are not too concerned with doing everything 'right' but rather with experiencing new behaviors and new reactions; later on each person can judge what best fits his or her own style and point of view."

Assign Participants Roles Other than Their Own. Often the best way of getting started is to ask a group member—after an appropriate warm-up—to play the role of a subordinate or someone with whom he or she interacts. For example, in the case of the teacher who described a difficult student, the facilitator might ask the teacher to play the role of the student. The facilitator might say, "You have worked with this student quite a bit; you seem clear about some of his difficulties and sources of his resistance. If you could portray the student for us it would give other people in the group a chance to work on a problem that they may have encountered themselves or may encounter in the future."

Have the Group Define Approaches Rather than Have Individuals Illustrate Their Own Techniques. Whenever an individual is asked to handle a problem to the best of his or her ability, a heavy element of evaluation and judgment is implied. Group members tend to say, "Here are some things you could have done better," or "I would have handled it differently"—implying that the person who handled the situation did not do it right. To avoid this trap the facilitator can ask the group members to define patterns of behavior and techniques or skills that can be experimented with in a role play. Rather than saying, "How would you handle the situation?" (thus asking a person to act out the role and submit to being evaluated), the facilitator can summarize or list various ways of handling the problem developed by the group and then ask people to try out these alternatives. Thus, the role player is not necessarily exhibiting the way he or she would act but rather is trying a role or pattern of behavior assigned by the group.

Use Role Rotation. Rather than centering on one person to play the key role and therefore focusing on that individual's skill, knowledge, or competency, it often is appropriate to have three or four people handle parts of the role and then discuss the total situation. This avoids direct criticism of one individual and provides linkages between various people who can supplement and complement each other as they experiment with a new situation. The facilitator can prepare people for this activity by saying, "Now we are going to try to deal with this troublesome student. I would like two or three people to try to talk to him and find out what is going on in terms of his resistance. Each person will have two or three minutes. Maybe in the next ten minutes or so we can find out more about the student and what he is feeling and *then* develop some new strategies for working with him."

Continue the Warm-Up During the Enactment. In a role-play session the connections between those in the enactment (in front of the room) and those observing (in the audience) should be maintained throughout the session. The facilitator should continue the warm-up by involving group members in the process. For example, the facilitator might say to the person playing the role of the counselor, "Why don't you try to find out a little bit about how this student sees things?" The interaction then might proceed for a short period, and the facilitator might intervene again to involve the audience: "Most of you have worked with students who are resistant to counseling or guidance. Does this student sound typical up to now?" Through this intervention the facilitator takes the focus away from an evaluation of the counselor and puts it on the student and the nature of the problem.

Using techniques that will be outlined later, the facilitator may then use a wide range of interventions to maintain connections between the rest of the group and the role players. *Role playing is effective when the members of the audience feel that they, too, are represented in front of the room rather than sitting in judgment on someone else's performance.* Similarly, the persons involved in the enactment are more apt to learn and become more open and spontaneous when they feel that they are part of the group—striving to understand the situation, experimenting with new ideas, and sharing information—rather than actors who are about to be reviewed and criticized by a psychologically distant audience.

Use Action Methods. Role playing facilitates learning through interaction. Once the participants have been chosen, it is important to move into enactment quickly. Background information should be minimized at this point; the facilitator should set "action" situations.

In reviewing developmental role playing it becomes clear that the process is relatively spontaneous and creative. At some point the facilitator may stop the action to interview the target role player (the counselor in the case we have provided) in order to find out more about how he or she is feeling and then check with the members of the audience to determine whether they, too, have shared some of these feelings. At other times, if the audience is supportive and the role players are becoming free and spontaneous, the facilitator may let the role play run for a while and then move into the post-enactment discussion. The facilitator also may have people reverse positions or rotate roles or may use new people to act out the problem situation. Three or four people may be asked at various times to play the roles of difficult students and three or four other members asked to try counseling those students.

As people become more and more involved in the process, it may be desirable to summarize principles, techniques, or key theoretical ideas that will be useful to the group as it digs more deeply into the issues. The facilitator may use the enactment to extract new ideas and to codify techniques and principles that emerge from the session. The group may be divided into smaller units for multiple role playing so that the members can experiment with counseling problems in a less high-pressure, large-group situation. Because of the wide range of options available in developmental role playing, it is extremely difficult to predict the outcome of such a session.

It is desirable in many organizational settings to use structured situations and enactments to obtain predictability, to aid group members in developing skill and knowledge, and to enable participants to feel comfortable and at ease in role-play situations. Within this context, an unstructured session may occasionally be interjected, or—if the facilitator feels comfortable and confident working with a given group over a relatively long period of time—the session may gradually become increasingly unstructured as people become more experimental, more open, and more spontaneous in relating to interpersonal or organizational problems.

FEEDBACK

Sources of Feedback

People do not necessarily learn from experience. In activities such as baseball, tennis, drawing, or public speaking, performance does not necessarily improve by simply repeating the activity. The vast majority of people learn and improve primarily through obtaining instruction and feedback. Based on that feedback, practice and continual application of what has been learned are critical to improvement.

The post-enactment analysis is in large measure a feedback process. After the enactment of the role play is completed, the facilitator may intervene in order to obtain observations, reactions, or guidance from group members. At times the post-enactment discussion may not occur until the end of an entire sequence of role playing. It is important that the facilitator explain and establish that feedback and other forms of post-enactment analysis are aimed at providing new insights, new opportunities, and support, rather than evaluation.

Feedback from Performance or Results. If a facilitator runs a training session, and the participants report high levels of satisfaction and are seen to perform better as a result of the training, the facilitator has received positive feedback from the situation itself, from the results achieved. A person who does not achieve positive results in a given situation is also getting feedback. In this case the person needs to re-examine his or her performance and determine what additional steps must be taken in order to achieve good results. It may be necessary for the individual to solicit more systematic feedback or to observe others in similar situations so that his or her performance can be improved by the use of proven techniques and approaches. In role playing, as in many other endeavors, feedback may come from actual performance.

Feedback Against Standards or Criteria. It is not always possible to obtain feedback based on results alone. For example, classroom teachers have difficulty judging their own effectiveness because the competencies, motivations, and backgrounds of their students vary so greatly. Thus, a teacher whose students do well on tests is not necessarily better than a teacher whose students do not test well. There are often many other variables that need to be considered. It frequently may be necessary, therefore, to establish criteria other than, or in addition to, bottom-line results. It is also often true that inability to obtain bottom-line results may be because of performance problems or other factors that need to be identified clearly and then improved before they can contribute to basic objectives.

For example, performance regarding patient care in one section of a hospital may be much lower than in another section. It may be measured by patient reactions, mistakes made in dispensing medication, and other specific criteria. However, the hospital personnel in the first section may not know how to improve the quality of patient care even though they are aware that their section is not doing as well as others. It may be necessary to isolate a variety of measurable performance criteria in order to achieve a broader objective in examining patient care. The nurses may need feedback on medication practices; aides may need training in interpersonal skills and other dimensions of their relationships with patients. In another example, to tell a sales representative "You are not making enough sales" may be inadequate feedback to aid that person in improving his or her per-formance. It may be necessary to identify specific performance factors such as sales prospecting, the ability to handle objections, the ability to close the sale, and so on. In applying this approach to role playing, the facilitator must establish—or engage the group in establishing—performance criteria for the procedure or skill being practiced.

Impressionistic Feedback. In many situations it is almost impossible to develop "hard" criteria for measuring performance and providing feedback. For example, a fund raiser may follow all the prescribed rules in dealing with potential donors but something may be lacking. A casual observer might say, "I get the impression that you really don't enjoy your job," or "It seems to me you just aren't enthusiastic," or "I don't think you are a very good listener." In many cases it is possible to convert these impressions into more tangible and specific performance criteria. However, in many situations impressions, perceptions, and reactions are just as important as hard data. If, for example, a subordinate gives a manager the impression that the subordinate is hostile or resentful, it really does not matter very much whether it is a hard fact. The subordinate may think of himself as "shy" or "self-possessed," but others see him as "aloof" or "hostile." Role playing provides many opportunities for giving and receiving impressionistic feedback. Since many such impressions can stand in the way of effectiveness and success, the information received from this feedback can be very valuable.

Data-Based Feedback. There are numerous ways to make feedback more accurate and less impressionistic. All involve some structured methods for recording what the role player does. This can be done by an observer, using a written observation guide (see Appendix 2 for a sample). A written questionnaire can be administered to the role players and observers during the role play, after the role play, or at several times. The most complete feedback can be provided by recording the role players' behaviors on audio- or videotape. These media, however, are overrich in feedback data, so the facilitator must be skilled in using them as feedback tools. This means selecting specific "bits" of behavior and leading the group and the role player to valid insights. Although effective use of the tape media requires skill and practice on the part of the facilitator (see Francis & Young, 1979, for a detailed presentation), these are powerful feedback tools. It is difficult for a role player to deny or distort his or her own behavior when that behavior is being audibly or visually displayed.

While the tape-recording media require training for effective application, much can be done with observation guides and questionnaires. These methods generate valid data that can be very useful in providing feedback, especially when comparisons can be made among several role players or role-play groups, allowing participants to see their own behavior in the context of a range of behaviors.

The Nature of Feedback

Regardless of the source of feedback, its impact may be either positive or negative. When an individual hears that he or she has achieved desired results, has performed in accordance with expectations, or has created a good impression, in the vast majority of instances, a positive feeling is created. Such information is positive, supportive, and affirmative. If the reverse occurs, the individual is left feeling ineffective or diminished as a result of the feedback.

Regardless of the negative feelings that negative feedback may evoke, it is nonetheless necessary. A golfer who slices the ball receives negative feedback—the ball does not go where he wants it to go. The golfer may become angry, disgruntled, or discouraged as a result of his performance, but the feedback is unavoidable. Similarly, a person who hears that he or she is giving the impression of being aloof, hostile, or aggressive may be annoyed or troubled, but, nonetheless, the information needs to be dealt with in one way or another.

Some role-play feedback comes from the situation itself. The individual generally is aware that he or she did not accomplish the task or caused resistance or hostility in an interaction with another. However, one of the difficulties encountered in dealing with interpersonal issues is that individuals are not aware of their own impact or are so wrapped up in their own actions they fail to notice how these actions affect or appear to others. Therefore, after each role-play enactment or after a series of enactments, the facilitator should ensure that feedback occurs and that an opportunity is provided for the results of that feedback to be utilized and applied.

Structured Feedback Procedures

In structured role-play designs, which have predetermined goals and outcomes, feedback processes generally are designed into the overall process. This is done by specifying where, when, and how the feedback will occur. Typically, a problem situation is presented, members are assigned roles, and the instructions follow something like this:

> One member of your team will play the part of the manager and the other the part of the subordinate. After you have worked on the situation for about ten minutes, the observer assigned to your team will ask you to stop interacting. The observer then will review his or her notes and provide feedback so that all three members of your subgroup can discuss the effectiveness of the procedure and ways in which it might be applied in real-life situations.

In other instances, feedback is obtained by polling the group. For example, in multiple role-play sessions, formats are designed by which group responses can be tabulated. The facilitator may ask, "How many in the group feel that you would be willing to change your mind regarding the problem at issue, based on this discussion?" By analyzing similar questions, group members can gain more insight into group effectiveness, group dynamics, and leadership behavior.

Unstructured/Developmental Feedback Procedures

In developmental role-play sessions feedback is not specifically built into the process. Just as is the case in the climate-setting and action phases of the role play, the feedback or post-enactment phase emerges from group interests and group concerns. Rather than telling the group what to look for, the facilitator in developmental sessions may ask: "At what point did you feel most involved in this process?" "What was most interesting or stimulating to you?" "In what ways were you able to identify with the protagonist as he or she responded to the other individual?" Thus, group members give feedback, but rather than analyzing and evaluating the performance of others they have an opportunity to demonstrate their own empathy and their own concerns and identification with other members of the group who have interacted in a problem situation.

GENERALIZING

In both structured and unstructured role-play sessions, closure is necessary. Participants have in most instances been through a series of exercises and experiences that have suggested the possibility of changes in behavior, application of new techniques, and development of new ways of relating to others. It is usually desirable to make it possible for the participants to act upon these newly surfaced concerns and objectives. Post-enactment analysis is concerned for the most part with providing feedback to individuals and giving them some indication of new directions that might be possible in handling critical issues. It often is possible to organize this feedback experience into a more generalized form so that members feel they have a basis for acting both individually and in concert.

Clearly, a role-play training session is not an appropriate setting for developing new policy or procedures, although at times role playing may lead to follow-up activities that do produce policy or procedural changes. The appropriate focus for the close of a role-play endeavor is on action steps that can be taken within the areas of freedom and responsibility represented in the group.

Open-Ended Sessions

One possibility for ending a session is to leave future actions more or less open-ended with little attempt to specify alternatives or generalize about conclusions or techniques that emerged during the session. This open-ended termination of a session is occasionally useful when there is a series of sessions underway and when the facilitator and the group members wish to think over what has happened, let it "sink in" or "percolate," and follow it up in later sessions.

In addition, there may be times when there are simply no answers and the situation is truly open-ended. People then have to act on their own beliefs or take a wait-and-see approach. For example, in some role-play sessions that focus on assertiveness skills it becomes evident that participants are uncomfortable in expressing negative feelings to others and have not resolved their own approaches to defending themselves or striving toward their goals. Although assertiveness training theory and the facilitator's own biases may suggest a desired course of action, participants themselves may not yet have experienced situations or behaviors that are supportive of the theories or the methodology. Thus, a group member might say, "I found that when my boss puts me down, the best thing for me to do is shut up and take it." Another member might say, "I am not sure what I want to do in dealing with tough clients. I am simply not ready to be assertive with them. It just doesn't feel right to me." If these comments are made near the end of a session, the facilitator or group members might arrive at an open-ended conclusion: "Many of us in the group are not sure yet how we want to deal with our own assertive needs and drives. We need to have more experience together or simply think things over for a while before we decide on how we want to respond."

Even in situations where an open-ended approach occurs, there is still an action commitment: people agree that they will think the issues over or read about them or talk to friends and associates.

Another circumstance in which generalizing about desired behavior or specifying action steps is inappropriate is when the role-play experience has been highly individualized and emotional. There is simply no basis for prescribing behavior and no need to prescribe it. In an intensive role play an individual may become acutely aware of a need to follow a given procedure or behave in a new way. The need may be manifest in the individual's ongoing behavior, and the intensity of commitment may be quite clear. To impose generalizations, value judgments, or prescriptions on people who have developed their own commitments or are intensively involved in reassessing their own situations may well be presumptuous and, more dangerously, may preclude further learning or insight.

In summary, it is rarely desirable to force insights or information on individuals who are developing their own frames of reference and their own commitments to the issues at hand. An individual needs time to assimilate what has happened in his or her own terms, the opportunity to experiment independently, and some "psychological space" in which to make decisions without explicit or implicit pressure from the group or the facilitator.

Action Planning

In the vast majority of instances, closure of a role play should be specific and clear-cut. It usually is appropriate to involve the group members in extracting generalizations or learnings from the specific experiences that occurred during the role play. These generalizations then lead to more specific plans of action.

From Generalizations to Specifics

Often, through various forms of post-enactment analysis—observer guides, statistical polling of the group, personal reactions, and feedback from group members—it is possible to arrive at generalizations regarding the experiences that have occurred during the role play. For example, in a session on interviewing or counseling it may become clear that too much conversation from the interviewer tends to block effectiveness. The resulting generalization may be "It is usually inappropriate for you (the interviewer or counselor) to dominate the conversation." It may now be possible to develop specific methods, commitments, or courses of action, based on the role-play experience, that support the generalization. Toward this end, the facilitator may codify ideas gradually throughout the session or may bring these ideas together through group discussion at the end of the session to summarize possible action steps. For example, action plans agreed on at the end of the role play described above might include:

1. Rather than repeating your own opinion, ask questions to clarify the opinions of others.
2. After you have asked a question, remain silent for ten or fifteen seconds rather than reframing your question or trying to push the other person to talk.
3. Summarize the other person's point of view frequently to show that you are listening and to aid the person in expressing or clarifying his or her ideas.

In highly programed sessions, the generalizations that emerge can be converted into procedural form. For example, after a post-enactment analysis the facilitator might sum up a session on handling union grievances by saying, "Based on all your comments, we have concluded that union grievances should be handled in accordance with the procedures spelled out in the contract. Beyond that we have begun to identify ways in which the specific steps in a grievance procedure can be executed effectively." The facilitator would then summarize previously agreed-on action steps consistent with the procedure under discussion.

Generalizations About Principles

Very often a series of enactments and post-enactment discussions can clarify and support a general principle. The principle may be theoretical or a matter of practice or policy. For example, company policy or a union contract may indicate that an individual should not be terminated without being given ample warning and the opportunity to improve. The principle involved is one of "progressive discipline." That is, there is a progressive sequence of steps aimed at correcting the problem and these are appropriate disciplinary measures or developmental stages at each progressive level. In other words, people should not be fired on the spur of the moment and without prior knowledge of the conditions under which termination will occur, and, whenever possible, specific and continued attempts should be made to improve performance rather than to terminate an individual for inadequate performance.

After having role played a series of situations regarding termination practices, participants are often much more aware of the possible consequences of inappropriate disciplinary action. This awareness may be stated in terms of feelings and attitudes: "I now understand better what it feels like to be criticized for something when you did not even know that you were responsible for it." Or "Now I see why we can be in serious trouble if we fire people without adequate notice." Thus, the general principle of applying progressive discipline has been experienced in a way that makes it possible for the facilitator and the group to be much more specific about action steps that need to be taken and much clearer about the meaning of the principle.

Theoretical or human relations principles can be reinforced and understood more fully through role-play enactments followed by appropriate generalization. For example, one well-established (Maier et al., 1975) role play used in many settings deals with the way in which people react to change. Thousands of supervisors have participated in this structured role play, and the designer of the role play kept careful records of the reactions of people who went through the role-play process, which involves a change in work procedure. Role-play experience demonstrates that when people are asked to change a work procedure in a predetermined way, without being given alternatives or an opportunity to have their own ideas and thoughts considered, they will tend to resist the change.

Conversely, when role players are given a chance to examine alternatives and participate in the construction of the change procedure, they are much more supportive of that procedure. Through structured role play, supervisors in a wide range of organizations have discovered that work procedures are responded to more positively when the workers are provided with alternatives. A second principle closely related to the first is that changes in work procedures are received much more positively when employees feel that they have some impact on the change.

Generalizations About Skills

Many individuals believe that every person has a right to "do his or her own thing." This point of view can extend to the ways in which people deal with personal or professional situations: selling, teaching, counseling, dealing with conflict, etc. The difficulty is that although spontaneity and individuality often are critical to personal effectiveness, they also are often used as excuses for an individual to avoid examining his or her own behavior and becoming more aware of his or her own effectiveness. The fact is that in most interpersonal situations there are opportunities to apply predetermined and well-established skills. A public speaker must develop the capacity or skill to project his or her voice so that it can be heard in a large room. Although there is a great deal of leeway in terms of personal style, tone of voice and so on, a basic requirement is that the person speak so that he or she can be heard. If a microphone is used, it is essential that the speaker remain close enough to the microphone to make it useful. Similarly, in conducting a decision-making or problem-solving conference it is almost always necessary to provide an opportunity for individuals to express their opinions and clarify ideas. It is not enough for an individual to say "I have my own style of public speaking" or "I run conferences in my own way" if that individual is performing in ways that are not producing the desired results.

Role playing often creates a climate in which participants become more aware of their behavior and more aware of the need for new skills or competencies to achieve desired results. This often results in appropriate generalizations regarding specific skills. It is rare for a group, after having engaged in a role play or any given procedural matter, *not* to agree that there are some techniques that are universally applicable. The facilitator can point out that these techniques can be maintained or improved through feedback and practice.

Generalizations About Action Plans

Many role-play sessions can be ended appropriately by focusing on action steps that all group members agree are appropriate. In a session dealing with voluntary fund raisers, it became clear that many of the participants were planning to try to raise funds by making telephone calls to friends and neighbors. Over the years, experience in the voluntary fund-raising activity in which participants were involved had shown that persons who were approached face-to-face were much more apt to donate funds than those who were contacted on the telephone. Both the frequency and size of the contribution was increased by face-to-face contact. Through role playing—using a simulated telephone interchange—participants were able to experience and compare the effects of a telephone call in contrast to a face-to-face contact. Other supportive techniques were used to encourage members to examine various modes of approaching people face-to-face. Role-playing guides and descriptions also provided hard data regarding the experience of various organizations that used telephone solicitation rather than face-to-face contact.

As a result of these enactments and post-enactment discussions over a period of several sessions, all group members agreed that face-to-face contact was the appropriate approach to use. Secondly, they practiced the skills required to deal with face-to-face contact with increasing ease and effectiveness. Finally, toward the end of the series of sessions, participants made specific action commitments: candidates or prospects were listed, appointment times were made and agreed on, and all members agreed to make face-to-face contacts under the circumstances and criteria mutually agreed on. The effect was that the fund-raising drive was more successful than it had been in previous years.

The critical point of generalizing from learnings in this manner is that participants make a direct action commitment. In similar situations, sales representatives may make commitments regarding the number of calls or the use of tie-in sales techniques; counselors and interviewers may make commitments regarding the nature or length of interviews or their own openness regarding new applicants, minority groups, or other special-interest groups. Through role playing and discussion, production employees may make commitments regarding new work procedures, new quality-control methods, or new ways of relating to each other.

SUMMARY

The role-play process has been divided into four components: climate setting, action, feedback, and generalizing. The procedures and skills associated with the process fit into two main categories: those used with structured role playing and those used with developmental role playing. Although the procedures within these two categories are somewhat different, they do overlap and are interconnected. A highly structured and programed experience may also involve developmental or open-ended discussions. Similarly, a developmental process may, from time to time, include structured materials and experiences to facilitate the developmental process.

REFERENCES

Anonymous. Act it, learn it. *Business Week*, April 9, 1949, 96-103.

Bavelas, A. Role playing and management training. *Sociatry*, 1947, *1*, 183-191.

Francis, D., & Young, D. *Improving work groups: A practical manual for team building*. San Diego, CA: University Associates, 1979.

Liveright, A. A. Role playing in leadership training. *Personnel Journal*, 1951, 29,412-416.

Maier, N. R. F., Solem, A. R., & Maier, A. A. *The role-play technique: A handbook for management and leadership practice*. San Diego, CA: University Associates, 1975.

6

Techniques

An effective application of technique occurs when the technique facilitates the development of knowledge, skills, or attitudes that improve individual effectiveness or enhance members' ability to implement plans, policies, and sound organizational or interpersonal processes. In role playing, carefully constructed training designs may be used or techniques often can be improvised on the spot. Decisions about when and how a technique should be used are best made from a performance-based orientation.

As indicated earlier, when goals and objectives are predetermined and specific outcomes are delineated, the role-play design is structured with carefully constructed climate-setting, action, feedback, and generalizing procedures. When the learning experience is open-ended and experimental, the process is developmental, with the facilitator and participants often responding spontaneously to changing situations, inventing new ways of exploring issues, and developing insights into key areas of concern. Ultimately the facilitator applies techniques that either move participants toward agreed-on and predetermined goals or contribute to the discovery and exploration of new objectives and new modes of behavior.

However, it is often not possible to classify or categorize techniques and designs this simply. In a carefully structured role play it may be useful—because of the nature of the interactions between participants—for the facilitator to intervene and apply a technique or procedure that was not preplanned. Conversely, during a spontaneous, developmental session, it may become clear that there is a need for specific skill training, and the facilitator may use prestructured or predesigned exercises, cases, or enactments to facilitate developmental and experiential learning.

The most sensible way to approach the application of a technique is first to be clear about the technique itself and subsequently to determine when and how that technique can be applied. For the purpose of this discussion, techniques will be divided into two categories, although these categories will sometimes overlap. The first category, *unstructured or developmental techniques*, is comprised of well-established methods used most often in spontaneous and unstructured role-play sessions. These techniques can, however, often be programed into a highly structured and carefully planned design. These techniques require interventions by the facilitator. The second category, *structured techniques*, are those most often built into a prestructured activity and are *not* facilitator dependent. They are built into the learning process and in large measure are self-administered by small groups or teams, often in a multiple role-play setting.

UNSTRUCTURED OR DEVELOPMENTAL TECHNIQUES

Unstructured/developmental techniques, usually used in an unstructured role play, are woven into an ongoing and emerging learning experience and must be applied with imagination and in response to the dynamics of the situation.

Straight or Demonstration Role Playing

In the most common and frequent application of developmental role playing, two individuals are asked to enact a given scene or situation relevant to the defined purposes of the session or to emerging needs and interests identified by participants. As indicated earlier, a variety of warm-up techniques may be used: a problem census (asking members to identify key problems in the area under examination), a demonstration film or presentation that elicits involvement, or an introductory role play. Thus, straight or demonstration role playing can be used as a warm-up, a way of getting people involved in the process. For example, the session might proceed as follows:

Facilitator: Our purpose today is to discuss how you as customer representatives deal with service complaints and problems. I'd like several of you to demonstrate what a typical problem looks like, and then we can begin to explore various ways of dealing with it. Will someone give me an example of a recent service complaint?

Participant A (Customer Service Representative): Well, the most common complaint I get—and I just got one today—is late deliveries. This customer was irate and belligerent—very hard to handle.

The facilitator may pursue this issue and check for common concerns and consensus or may choose to use the situation as a point of departure for further examination.

Facilitator: There may be dozens of different problems we could choose; this one will give us a chance to look at the nature of the consumer representative's role and some of the problems we encounter. Role player A, would you select a member of the group who will take the part of the customer? Then you and "the customer" go into the other room while you give him or her a brief outline of the customer's behavior. Don't spell it out word for word, just one or two brief indications of how the customer behaved and how he or she responded when you dealt with the complaint.

When the two role players leave the room, the facilitator briefly outlines to the participants some of the aspects of the problem to be explored during the session. When the two participants return, the facilitator structures the session by making the situation as specific and realistic as possible. The basic procedure for getting the key player into the role is to ask specific questions. When, where, what, and how questions are essential to the warm-up process.

Facilitator: Okay, role player A, where were you when this happened?

Participant A responds, and the facilitator continues to pin down the time, the place, the general atmosphere, and more data about how the protagonist was feeling so as to recreate some of the feelings present in the original scene. The two role players then interact.

Customer (B): This is the third time I have called to try to get my order delivered. It is holding up work in our organization and it is costing us a lot of money. I don't understand why you people can't get on the ball!

Customer Service Representative (A): Well, I was not aware of the fact that the order was late until you called this morning, and we put a tracer on it. We do know that it has left our shipping room and is somewhere in transit. It left two days ago and was scheduled to arrive at your place yesterday.

B: Oh, really. That information doesn't do me any good. It's costing me money now and I hold your organization accountable for that.

Thus the straight or demonstration role play has begun. The facilitator may let it run for a while, or may ask other people to demonstrate similar interactions, or may begin working with the group to develop criteria or strategies for dealing with the situation. Alternatively, the facilitator may use a variety of techniques to contribute to the spontaneity and insight of both participants. A more or less standard procedure in developmental or spontaneous role playing is to use a specific interviewing technique sometimes referred to as *soliloquizing* or the *on-the-spot interview.* The purpose of the interview is to expose more clearly to all participants and observers what is going on in the situation—is it realistic, do the people involved understand each other's feelings, are there other ways in which they could become more clear and more direct?

Soliloquizing: The On-the-Spot Interview

Assume that the previous role play continues:

A: We are really doing the best we can. I can understand that you are upset about this, but I have made every effort to get the material to you as scheduled.

Now the facilitator may interrupt in order to validate the reality of the situation and/or to aid group members in developing more insight into what has occurred.

Facilitator: Role player A, is this pretty much the way it happened?

A: Yes, that's pretty close to the way the customer acted.

Facilitator: Tell me right now how you are feeling as you begin to try to protect the company's interests and to cool off the customer.

A: Well, even though it is part of my job to try to keep people happy, I do get kind of annoyed.

Facilitator: You find it annoying. Tell me more about that.

A: Well, once I have apologized a couple of times I find myself beginning to get angry, and I begin to feel like it is all right to accommodate the customer but I don't want to be pushed around.

At this point, the facilitator has a wide range of choices. He or she can explore further how role player A feels and what actions are taken based on those feelings. This raises questions about how the individual deals with his or her own anger or hostility and whether the role player successfully stays in touch with the customer or begins to alienate and create tensions with the customer. Alternatively, this is often a good spot to pause for support and reinforcement from the observers. The facilitator might ask the group, "How many of you have felt angry and upset when a customer berates you or argues about something when you feel you have done all you can?"

In any case, this interruption of the process is only temporary and is to ensure that the key participant feels that the situation is realistic and not simply a charade. Secondly, the interruption provides the opportunity for all members of the group to identify with the key role player and to obtain more insight into the feelings and reactions that occur in handling a situation of this type. Finally, the soliloquy or on-the-spot interview gives the facilitator a chance to introduce alternative approaches. For example, the facilitator might say, "What are some of the other ways in which you might draw this person out? Let's experiment with them."

Often it is appropriate to let the situation run for a while until both parties become further involved. On the other hand, if involvement is slow in developing, it may be necessary to interrupt and interview one or both of the role players to bring the situation into a clear focus and to ensure that participants and observers are in touch with the real issues. If there is lack of clarity or if the participants do not seem to be warming up very well, it is often useful to use a technique called *role reversal* or *switching*.

Role Reversal

Role reversal or switching occurs when one individual is asked to change positions with and take on the role previously being played by the other. For example, in the case used for illustration, role player A would be asked to change roles with role player B, the complaining customer. It is important to actually have the persons change positions so that the physical change encourages their mental or psychological change. Besides supporting the feeling that one is changing from one role to another, this also keeps the situation clear to those observing. For example, the chair on the right can always represent the auxiliary player (the customer).

Role reversal accomplishes one or more of the following objectives:

Clarifying the Situation. By switching roles it is possible for the key role player who knows the situation to demonstrate how it is handled by the other person. For example, in this case the only person in the room who has any knowledge of how the actual customer behaved is role player A. By putting A in the customer's chair, the group is able to get at least a representation of the customer as seen by A. In addition, this switching process gives all parties a chance to clarify the facts. Role player A in the customer's role can now be very specific about the complaint and can mirror the tone of voice and attitude of the customer.

Increasing Spontaneity. A second reason for using role reversal is to keep people moving and loose. Some people become "stuck" in their "usual" role and behave in a stereotyped or mechanical fashion. By changing roles they are to some degree shaken out of their stereotypes and are forced, through the process itself, to re-examine what is going on from different perspectives and to try out different behavior.

Increasing Insight and Awareness. Often a simple role reversal makes one or both of the parties much more aware of how the other person is feeling, and the subsequent enactment brings to light some of the feelings and behaviors that might not otherwise have been identified. The following is an example of various ways of using the role-reversal technique in combination with on-the-spot interviews to increase insight and spontaneity and to clarify the facts and issues in the situation.

When asked whether the customer was portraying the part accurately, role player A said, "No, the customer was much more belligerent than that." The facilitator could proceed as follows:

Facilitator: I suggest that you change seats with the customer. Become the customer and demonstrate to us how he actually behaved. Use his tone of voice and attitudes and clear up any of the facts that need to be cleared up. Meanwhile, role player B, you are to move into the chair of the customer service representative and play the role pretty much as A has been playing it. Respond to the situations that arise as much as you can as member A has been responding. You may have to improvise and try out new things in order to deal with this customer.

The two role players then reverse seats.

Customer (now played by A): Now, look, I think your company is irresponsible and you are untrustworthy. You promised me the material would be delivered and you didn't live up to it.

Customer Service Representative (now played by B): Well, I have checked the order through, and it did go out three days ago. It was supposed to have arrived at your place yesterday. I'm sorry this has happened, but as you can see I have done everything possible to straighten it out.

The facilitator now intervenes and interviews A in his or her new role as the customer. This is done for the reasons outlined earlier (to clarify the situation, enhance spontaneity, and develop insight); however, the major focus in this instance is to increase insight.

Facilitator: Let me interrupt, A. How do you feel right now while the service representative is telling you that everything possible has been done and that the material has been checked out and was supposed to be delivered yesterday?

A: I feel B is making excuses; B's not trying to help me solve my problem, he's telling me his problems.

Thus, by playing the role of customer, A (the protagonist) becomes more aware of the customer's concerns and suspicions and may develop some insight into the customer's feelings and motives. Typically, when an initial insight occurs and when the situation is clarified, it is appropriate to have the persons involved return to their own roles. So the facilitator may say, "I think you have clarified the customer's actions and reactions and perhaps you have a little better knowledge of how the customer may have been feeling and thinking when you were talking. Please change back now and resume your original roles."

Rather than forcing the insight, the facilitator lets the situation continue. Having been in the role of the customer, the customer service representative may now try a new approach. The role play continues with the facilitator getting the players back into their roles and giving A a chance to begin practicing new behavior by asking the customer to repeat the complaint.

Facilitator: "Okay, member B, now that you have heard the real customer, why don't you make the complaint pretty much as it actually was made."

Note that the facilitator validates that the situation is real rather than referring to it as hypothetical.

B (back in the role of customer): Well, as I told you, you are causing me a lot of trouble. It's embarrassing to me, and I'm losing money, and I expect you to do something about it.

A (back in the role of customer service representative): I certainly understand that you are upset, and I would like to review with you what steps are available to us. Of course, one thing I can do is try to send out another shipment right away in case the first one is lost. However, we did put a tracer on that first shipment and we know it's en route. Is there any kind of help I can give you while we are trying to trace it further?

And so the role play continues, with both parties having had the experience of being in the other's role and of gaining a little more insight into the nature of the problem from another's point of view.

It should be noted that role reversal or switching is one of the most powerful role-play techniques. Very often policemen have never been offenders, nurses have never been patients, and teachers may have forgotten the role of student. Similarly, the first time that a supervisor plays the role of a union representative attempting to settle a grievance for an angry employee, he or she may gain new insight into the pressures on the union steward. By moving from role to role in various situations, group members increase their flexibility, their awareness of a wider range of attitudes, and their responses and concerns, and generally enhance their ability to interact more freely and openly within changing situations.

Doubling

A supplemental technique similar to soliloquy is the doubling technique. This occurs when a third individual is brought into the role-play situation and is asked to become the "inner voice" of one of the role players. The facilitator introduces the idea. "When one is involved in interactions with others, one often has a lot of things going on in his mind that he either does not care to express or does not have time to express. Our minds and our feelings work much faster than our words can respond. Therefore, we are going to add another person to this situation to express the unexpressed thoughts and feelings of one of the players."

This technique requires quite a bit of direction and prodding from the facilitator since it is new to participants and they frequently do not understand it at first. One option in this instance is for the facilitator to assume the doubling role the first time to demonstrate how it works. A second option is for the facilitator periodically to interrupt the interaction to interview the "inner voice" of one of the major role players. For example, continuing with the previous case illustration, let us assume that additional tensions begin to develop.

A: Well, I think I have suggested every alternative I can put my finger on, but nothing seems to satisfy you. It was a misdelivery. It was a mistake. We are doing everything we can to correct it. I just don't know what else I can do.

Just prior to this point the facilitator had placed a double with player B (the person playing the role of the customer). First, the primary role player B speaks.

B: Well, for one thing, you can stop making promises you can't keep and stop lying to me about the delivery schedule.

At this point the facilitator intervenes and directs the group's attention to the person playing the double (the inner voice or conscience of the customer).

Facilitator (looking at the double for B): You seem to be very antagonistic. Nothing seems to satisfy you. What do you really want from this person? Why are you so angry and belligerent?

B (double): I get these stories all the time. All these vendors are the same. They make promises they can't keep, and this one is no better than the rest of them.

Facilitator: The customer service representative put a tracer on the order, has told you where it stands, seems to have given you evidence to support the situation, and has even apologized. What more do you want?

B (double): Well, I don't know. All I know is that I am going to get hell from my boss. I am very upset and concerned about this; there's no out for me at all. The material isn't here, it's embarrassing, and I'm the one on the spot.

Facilitator: And so because of this you feel that your best approach is to be as nasty as you can with the vendor?

B (double): Well, not nasty, but I want to let the vendor know how badly this has affected me.

Facilitator: What could the vendor do that would make you feel better?

Note that the facilitator, by asking these questions—encouraging B's double to soliloquize—is also calling attention to some possible positive actions that might be taken. The facilitator may then encourage all three participants to continue the enactment with the double interrupting periodically to express the customer's unexpressed thoughts.

There is a variation of the doubling technique. Just as straight role playing concerns itself with the representation of action, the doubling technique can be a representation of contemplation. To demonstrate this application, a different example will illustrate how a problem that is not readily dramatized can be clarified and intensified through the use of doubling. The facilitator introduces the problem and, in this instance, takes on the role of the double. Thus, when the real A speaks it is shown in the script as A (A). When the double speaks, it is shown in the script as A (facilitator). In the new situation, two department heads are in conflict.

Facilitator: When we have a problem, we usually try to think around it, see it from every point of view, explore the pros and cons. Let us use a new technique to explore a department head's (role player A) problems and concerns. I will play A the first time to show you how the method works. Later on you may want to try it in other situations. A, I will be your other self and will think along with you. I will imitate your motions and actions and will try to think as you do. If I go off the track, correct me. If you agree with the things that I am saying, support them or extend them, but do not permit me to act or behave in any way that is not consistent with your own feelings. As I understand your situation, you are concerned about talking to another department head about that person's lack of cooperation with you. Start the discussion by expressing your ideas about how to deal with this person.

A (A): *I am really fed up with the lack of cooperation from the people in department X. They seem to feel like they are competitors instead of members of the same organization.*

A (facilitator): *I really get angry about this. I would like to tell the head of that department what I think of him.*

A (A): *I have been tempted several times but I know that you can't accomplish much by fighting with people.*

A (facilitator): *I guess the best thing is to try to smooth things over and not rock the boat.*

A (A): *I suppose that is what I have been doing—not rocking the boat. I do feel that this person is taking advantage of the situation.*

A (facilitator): *Of course, if I confront him about it he will probably get angry and give me a hard time.*

A (A): *I'm sure he will. He is one of those people with a short fuse, and I just don't like to deal with people who blow up all the time.*

A (facilitator): *I guess the best thing to do is just go along with it. It is annoying, and he walks over me quite a bit, but the main thing is to keep things running smoothly.*

A (A): *Well, I don't like being walked over. I really think I should talk to him.*

A (facilitator): *I think I'll say, "Look, why don't you wise up and stop acting like we are on different teams? I can play that game too."*

A (A): *Not only that, but I am sick and tired of being pushed around.*

A (facilitator): *Yet even as I'm saying these things, I don't feel comfortable about this. I can just sense myself getting into a fight, and I hate fights.*

A (A): *Maybe what I ought to do is be straightforward about it but not belligerent. Maybe I should say something like, "Let's sit down and talk about how we can cooperate better."*

A (facilitator): *But I don't want to be too wishy-washy. I want to let him know that there is a real problem but at the same time not be hostile. I don't know, sometimes I think I would like to be hostile.*

A (A): *Well, I certainly feel angry, but I don't think that is the answer. I think the thing to do is to be straightforward, give him the facts, and hang in there until I get the thing straightened out. What I have to do is get across to him the problem and just refuse to engage in name-calling. If I'm straightforward and firm, I'm sure I can get the thing settled.*

There are many ongoing applications of this technique. It is a way of warming up people to begin a role play. It is particularly useful in sales training in pointing out how the salesperson gets ready to make a call. By placing a double with a salesperson and having the two explore their feelings (particularly if both persons are really sales representatives), one can teach them to build confidence and get ready for action more effectively.

Sales Representative A: Well, it is tough to make a cold call on a customer like this, but I guess I have to do it.

Sales Representative B: Not only do I have to do it but it's a way to make money.

Sales Representative A: And my experience shows that if you go in there with a positive attitude and present the product clearly, the chances are that you will get a positive reaction.

Sales Representative B: I know that I have a good product and I am a persuasive, convincing person. I'm going in there with a positive frame of mind.

Facilitator: Okay, here is Mr. X, a tough resistant customer. Try out your approach on him, and the rest of us will observe. Later on each of us can try out a similar experience.

Finally, the doubling technique can be used in a slightly different form called "group doubling." In this instance, the entire group or portions of the group are asked to express the inner thoughts or unexpressed thoughts or feelings of one or more role players.

For example, if two teachers have just demonstrated a disciplinary interaction between a teacher and a student, the facilitator will divide the group in half so that half the participants would serve as "double" for the teacher and the other half would double for the student. The facilitator then might say, "Now I would like all the 'teachers' to express some of your feelings and reactions to the student as a result of the disciplinary discussion you just held. Make your statements brief, feel free to step in and interrupt each other, get your ideas out on the table. We may at times have more than one person talking at once, but in many cases that is the way our minds work when we are in complicated situations." After the teacher doubles have expressed their views, the facilitator would say, "Now let's hear how the student doubles feel."

At times this technique can be turned back into straight role playing by having one of the students and one of the teachers continue the discussion in front of the group. Often the emotion of the real-life situation is strengthened by the doubling process.

The Mirror Technique

In the mirror technique, the individual does not take on the role of the inner voice of another; rather, the individual takes on the role of another and portrays it to mirror back to the protagonist how he or she appears.

The second application of the mirror technique is used to engage people in role playing who are resistant to becoming involved in the process. Assume that participant A has talked quite a bit about how she would handle a demanding professional associate who was not cooperative (for example, how a nurse or paramedical person might deal with a hostile or overbearing doctor). However, when A is asked to demonstrate her approach, she may resist. The facilitator would then say, "Since member A would rather not portray the role of the paramedic dealing with the senior staff officer, perhaps someone else will play the role as A has described it. Member A, is that all right with you?" Participants almost always agree to let someone else play their roles, at least early in the session. The facilitator then calls on someone to take on the role of A, and A is encouraged to suggest ways in which the situation could be handled differently. Thus, role player A becomes involved and often interrupts the interaction to suggest different ways of behaving. It is not at all unusual for A finally to volunteer to demonstrate some of her ideas in a role play.

The mirror technique has many other variations. After small-group discussion or confrontation, members of the group can be asked to portray each other. This is done by changing everyone's role: A becomes B, B becomes C, and so on. A simpler version of the technique is to ask two or three people to show another person how he or she has acted in a given situation by mirroring that behavior. If only one person is singled out to be mirrored, it can be embarrassing and evoke tension. However, in the spontaneous role play, if from time to time different individuals are asked to mirror back to others, the technique can gain acceptance in the group and become a way of communicating perceptions and feelings without attacks or negative feedback. In several techniques to be described later (behavior rehearsal and behavior modeling), participants can learn how to portray a role more effectively by mirroring a more experienced person (or a filmed presentation of an appropriate procedure or style).

The Empty Chair Technique

At times a group member may have difficulty interacting with another individual because he or she is so preoccupied with trying to relate to and impress that person that the group member becomes awkward or finds it difficult to react. If an empty chair is used to simulate the other person, it takes the pressure off the protagonist. He or she does not have to be concerned about how the chair responds. At the same time, the group member can gain the experience of trying to deal with the other person. Often the empty chair technique leads to other interactions in which someone is asked to move into the chair and portray the symbolic role that has not yet been revealed. Or the protagonist may choose to move into the chair. This leads to still another technique.

The Self-Role-Play or Monodrama

Often an individual can gain insight into a given interaction by playing both roles, by literally switching between two chairs. Thus, the individual plays the role of the supervisor and then shifts to the role of the subordinate. The subordinate answers the supervisor and then returns to the supervisor's chair again. It takes some experience and practice to make this technique effective, but it is widely used in developmental role playing and with some experimentation can be very useful.

Shifts in Physical Position

Communication problems or relationships can be dramatized by changing physical positions. One example is for a person playing the part of a dissatisfied customer to gradually turn his or her back to the salesperson to indicate the opinion that the salesperson is not truly listening to the objection or complaint. Another variation is to have one individual stand while the other remains seated in order to dramatize a hierarchical or authoritarian relationship. Frequently the facilitator interviews the person seated in the chair, asking, "What is your reaction to having X standing up looking down at you?" Shifts in physical position, moving chairs farther apart or closer together, or having group members shake hands or make physical contact during an interaction are ways of dramatizing or demonstrating various levels in the interaction process.

Role Rotation

At times it is useful to move a series of people quickly through one role. For example, an individual may be asked to play the part of an angry citizen talking to a public official. Those being trained to be more effective in the role of public official may be asked in sequence to move into the role of the public official as the angry citizen continually makes the same complaint. Thus, in a very brief time, ten or fifteen people can experience the role and give a one- or two-sentence response to the angry citizen. This technique has two purposes. One is to elicit a wide range of responses; people can compare approaches and develop new awareness of the range of possibilities available to them. Second, role rotation often is a useful warm-up technique, allowing people to try new approaches and experiment with new behavior.

On-the-Spot Inventions

In developmental role playing, where there is no predetermined structure and system, often it is possible and useful for the facilitator and group members to improvise new ways of gaining insight or improving skills. For example, if an individual in the group is having trouble being firm or forceful with a resistant person, the facilitator may ask the group to suggest experiments that the individual could try in order to come across more forcefully. Someone might say, "Why don't you try pointing your finger at the person? I'm not suggesting that you should do this all the time, but it might give you a feeling of firmness." Someone else might suggest, "Why don't you try leaning forward a little bit? You seem to be rocking back on your heels." Another might suggest, "Why don't you try repeating your statement three or four times to convince yourself that it is the right statement and to have a stronger impact on the person you are dealing with?" In an open, spontaneous session people find ways of assisting each other to learn, to experiment, and to explore their own potential and develop their own resources.

In summary, there is a wide range of unstructured techniques, some of which have been used in many situations over a long period of time: role reversal, doubling, and the mirror technique are three. Many other techniques emerge as the facilitator and group members search for new ways of relating to each other and new ways of solving problems and producing results.

STRUCTURED TECHNIQUES

Structured role playing has been defined as role playing in which there are predetermined objectives and in which roles, background information, and procedures have, for the most part, been planned and designed prior to the session. One of the characteristics of the structured approach to role playing is that it does not rely on spontaneous interventions. Many role-play programs can be conducted by inexperienced trainers, and many designs are utilized by educational groups, voluntary agencies, industrial organizations, and various social groups without employing professional consultants or trained staff members. In addition, structured designs often are part of broader programs that may include other training devices, lectures, small-group discussions, and so on. The basic procedure for designing a structured role play is outlined in Chapter 4. The specific *techniques* associated with the design are as follows.

Multiple Role Playing

The most common form of the structured approach is multiple role playing. Small groups are provided with the same role-play assignment and simultaneously act out the situation. In most instances the process is programed: specific objectives are defined, time frames are indicated, and formats are used to elicit specific areas of concern and to provide a common focus for discussion. The techniques that facilitate and energize this type of role playing are quite different from those used in developmental sessions. Although it is possible to include a role reversal or the mirror technique, these would be unusual interventions in the structured role-play process.

Built-In Tension

Whether a role play is conducted as a demonstration or in a multiple format, the core of the structured approach is in the design itself and is therefore often difficult to identify. The energizing force in making structured role plays work is *built-in tension*. For example, if managers are being trained in performance-review techniques and are asked to role play a performance interview, the design is apt to fail if it includes no areas of disagreement or tension. There are several types of tension or conflict-building devices that can be used in designing a structured role play.

Conflict or Contradiction in Information. People can be given conflicting background or role information to cause tension. However, this information must be realistic and resolvable when further explored and exposed. For example, in a performance-appraisal role play the subordinate might be instructed: "You have had quite a few complaints from customers lately. The basic cause of these complaints is a new system that was installed by the engineering staff. The system is admittedly experimental, and though your boss was told about it in general, she was never given the specifics of the new approach. You feel you did all you could to resolve the causes of complaints. You did not want to put too much pressure on the engineers. You felt that your boss would have said something if she had wanted you to take a stand."

Concurrently, the instructions for the supervisor's role might include: "You are aware of the fact that your subordinate has been getting a lot of complaints. This is in part due to a new engineering approach. You feel that your subordinate should have been more assertive in not letting this approach get out of hand and causing dissatisfaction on the part of customers."

Conflicts in Immediate Past Experience. In handling a problem regarding a union representative, differences in experience are built into the management roles to provide a basis for examining management problem-solving approaches.

Supervisor A: Your contacts with the union steward have been rather unpleasant. He is extremely belligerent and evasive when it comes to pinning down issues. On the other hand, when someone from top management is around he tends to clam up. As you see it, his approach is to not let the people upstairs know that he is a troublemaker. You are not sure why he behaves this way, but it is bothersome.

Top Manager: You have been dealing with union steward X for quite a while, and he is not at all troublesome. He really is a rather quiet, retiring person. Yet you are constantly hearing that there is bickering between your supervisor and the steward. You simply don't understand it. It is hard for you to believe that the steward behaves belligerently. You really don't know what the problem is.

Note that in both of these brief examples, the issue causing tension is not necessarily true or false. The purpose of introducing conflicting perceptions in a performance-review design is to encourage participants to specify bottom-line performance goals and to determine ways of measuring whether those goals have been achieved.

Differences in Role or Responsibilities. Any number of management and organizational problems occur because individuals have loyalties to a given group or department. For example, in a university it is not at all unusual for the liberal arts department to encounter difficulties in resolving differences with other components of the university. In a structured role play designed to involve people in interdisciplinary development activities, the problem can be dramatized by building conflict into two roles.

Liberal Arts Professor: You are very much in favor of an interdisciplinary approach to education, and the dean of your college supports that idea. She feels, however, that the heart of all education is liberal arts, that liberal arts should be the major focus in undergraduate years, and that people should then move on into professional or technical disciplines. You are a member of a small committee trying to work out an interdisciplinary curriculum. You and your associates agree that a minimum of two years of liberal arts should precede any kind of professional or specialized education.

Professor of Mathematics: You are part of the faculty of the school of engineering. Many liberal arts students appear in your classes. You think that a good mathematician or a good engineer must have a liberal arts background in order to be a "whole person." On the other hand, you do not think that liberal arts prerequisites should be built into the curriculum. It is your experience that engineers, mathematicians, and other technical people are able to select key areas for their own learning and they should have a lot of freedom in choosing these areas. The main thing is that they know their disciplines, that they have met their prerequisites for moving forward in their chosen fields. As far as you are concerned, half a dozen or so liberal arts courses of their own choice are enough.

Differences in Objectives. Conflict can be induced easily in a group situation by providing people with different objectives. For example, in business game simulations and in many social and problem-solving simulations, tension is created simply by saying, "Your goal is to maximize the profitability of your unit." In a zero-sum situation, if team A maximizes its own profitability it means diminishing the profitability of others. Such intergroup tension and conflict in the role-play enactment provides the basis for feedback, skill development, and practice.

Built-In Resolution

It is not sufficient simply to build conflict or tension into a designed role play. Opportunities also must be provided for resolution of that conflict. This is achieved by including explicit or implicit options for resolution.

In their book, *The Role-Play Technique*, Maier, Solem, and Maier (1975) provide many illustrations of how various ideas and resistances can be integrated into appropriate solutions. The structured role plays designed by Maier have built-in tensions and opportunities for argument and defensiveness. However, in every instance, if the persons involved explore the problem in an appropriate fashion (i.e., if they look for alternatives, examine the situational context, avoid yes-no positions) their chances of successful resolution are great. For example, the book includes a structured case in which clerical staff members are accused of making too many phone calls. If the discussion leader or manager attempts to find out what each person is doing wrong, failure will follow. The authors sum up the objective of the process in a way that is typical of structured role playing:

> It is apparent that problems stated in situational terms are the most likely to prevent defensive reactions and the most likely to contain a mutual interest. However, interest in problem solving might cause some employees to become critical of others. It is at such times that the leader must protect the individual who is attacked. She can point out that the aim is to solve the problem in a manner suitable to all, that there are bound to be differences in values and viewpoints, and that the purpose of the discussion is to understand and resolve the differences. . . . At all times the leader's job is to keep the discussion situation-oriented and to respect differences in needs, values, and attitudes. (pp. 118-119)

Maier et al. proceed to prove this conclusion in a role-play exercise that summarizes the success of various groups and shows that when groups (and their managers) are situation oriented and willing to approach the problem in an open fashion, they are successful in their own terms (they feel good about the results) and in terms of the feasibility of their solutions.

SUMMARY

Two types of role-play techniques are available to the role-play facilitator. *Developmental or unstructured techniques* are used to facilitate the training group's involvement in an innovative, emerging process of learning. Role reversal, soliloquy, doubling, and other action methods are injected into the role play as it unfolds. Materials and techniques are not predetermined. *Structured techniques* focus on predetermined goals, training materials, and formats. Multiple role playing often is used to engage group members in concurrent enactments so that principles and relationships can be clarified and skills can be practiced. Often structured and unstructured methods are combined in a series of sessions, or within one session, to provide opportunities for learning through experimentation, discovery, and innovation as well as through systematic, organized enactments and discussions.

REFERENCE

Maier, N. R. F., Solem, A. R., & Maier, A. A. *The role-play technique: A handbook for management and leadership practice.* San Diego, CA: University Associates, 1975.

APPLICATIONS

7

Informing

Growing technology, increased organizational complexity, and the development of new management techniques have brought an increased need for information. Administrators need more data on which to base decisions. Employees need communication concerning organizational programs and policies. Managers need more facts about new techniques of management. Changes in methods, procedures, and systems must be communicated. In the modern organization the process of instructing and informing never ceases.

APPLICATIONS OF DEMONSTRATION ROLE PLAYING

Role playing can be used to inform and instruct in almost every situation in which films, lectures, and demonstrations are suitable. Effective human relations, safety practices, interviewing procedures and, in fact, any skill or principle that involves interaction between people, can be demonstrated through role playing.

Safety. An instructor in a safety program wishes to show the students why people frequently resist using safety aids such as goggles, machine guards, or safety helmets. Instead of merely talking about typical employee reactions to accident prevention devices, the instructor prepares several group members to act out one or more situations. They may be provided with "skeleton" scripts and told to fill in the dialog or the instructor may briefly explain their roles to them before the session. The role play is used to dramatize the situation. The group members observe the enactment in the same way that they would observe any audiovisual presentation, but the role play produces more interest and discussion than a lecture or a printed summary of the problem.

Interviewing. A lecturer wishes to explain the nondirective interviewing process to her audience. She finds it hard to explain how to conduct a nondirective interview. She sets up a hypothetical problem and has several assistants act it out. Now she can continue the lecture with specific reference to the interview that her audience has just witnessed.

Labor Relations. An industrial relations director sets up a new procedure for handling employee complaints and grievances. He finds that when he tries to explain the procedure to managers, he has difficulty holding their attention. He develops a realistic role play of a grievance situation. The role play is entertaining and provocative; it raises procedural questions for which the managers do not have answers. Once the director has engaged the attention and interest of his audience through role playing, he can lead them in exploring procedures and answering some important questions.

Role playing can be used as an audiovisual technique. Although much of the audience remains passive, the enactment attracts and focuses attention, stimulates interest, and dramatizes an interpersonal situation.

Information-giving role playing can be used to increase understanding of a fairly complex problem. For example, a group of field salespeople have been accepting orders that are difficult for the production department to fill. Because of their lack of understanding of the company's production operations, the salespeople have permitted customers to order nonstandard items that do not fit established manufacturing specifications. They also have promised unrealistic delivery dates.

The salespeople are invited to attend a series of training sessions. The first session opens with a lecture by the production manager, who briefly reviews the manufacturing process. Slides are used to illustrate key manufacturing operations. To dramatize a typical problem, some of the production people role play the handling of a sales order. The salespeople witness the demonstration but do not take part. They see the manufacturing superintendent approach a manager to tell him that an order has just been received for one thousand units of product X. The field salesperson in the role play has accepted minor changes in specifications for the product and has promised delivery in two weeks. The audience hears that the specification changes will require retooling of a substantial part of the equipment. This will result in a great deal of machine "down time." To meet the delivery date it will be necessary for many of the production workers to work overtime. The manager points out that he will have to hold up another order if the superintendent wants him to get this one out on time. The salespeople watch the two production people struggle with problems of scheduling, machine "down time," overtime costs, and the effect of the production specification change on the morale of the work force. They see, too, that another order must be held up to meet the special requirements of this one.

The goal of the session is to increase the sales force's understanding and knowledge of problems created by their behavior. The ultimate objective is to produce changes in the way the salespeople handle orders in the field. The discussion between the manager and the superintendent has more impact on the audience than pages of facts and figures documenting the cost of handling special sales orders.

These examples illustrate how information-giving role playing focuses attention, stimulates interest, and increases understanding. Its uses can be broken down more specifically into three categories: (a) to increase general understanding and knowledge, (b) to teach specific methods, and (c) to prepare for training.

Increasing General Understanding

The purpose of instruction is to change behavior. When information about "principles of human relations" or "safety practices" is communicated, the goal is to improve the way in which group members handle human relations or safety problems. There are situations, however, in which the goal of information-giving is less specific. For example, a company may wish to increase its employees' understanding of collective bargaining. The employees may be invited to attend a mock negotiation session in which members of the union and management act out a hypothetical collective-bargaining situation. Although the general goal of the session is to increase the employees' sense of involvement in management-union relations and to help improve communications between union members and supervisors, no specific behavioral change is anticipated. Nevertheless, some generalized improvement in the way in which employees react and respond to union-management problems may be expected.

Teaching Specific Methods

There are many situations in which management must require employees to conform to an established policy or legal requirement. For example, bank tellers must be instructed in basic procedures relative to check cashing, deposits, and withdrawals. A role play can be used to show the new teller how to conduct banking transactions.

Preparing for Training

Finally, information-giving or instructional role playing may be used to prepare a group for action training. The use of a new procedure can be demonstrated through role playing. The demonstration does not directly change the behavior or actions of the trainees, but it does prepare them to participate in action-learning situations that will, hopefully, result in more effective behavior.

There are a great many situations in which basic understanding must precede the development of skills and techniques. The communication of principles, theories, and proven methods often can be made more effective through role playing. In such cases role playing can increase the impact of rather dry material by dramatizing it.

SUMMARY

In any situation in which the goal is to demonstrate, emphasize, or clarify a principle, method, or complex set of facts involving interaction between people, role playing is useful.

The actors in a role play serve as living audiovisual aids. Unlike role players in a training or testing situation, participants in an information-giving session do not act spontaneously but are limited by the role instructions. Nor is the audience expected to move into action. Its role is to look and listen, to learn through observation.

Role playing to communicate information can often succeed in attracting attention, stimulating interest, and provoking discussion in situations in which more didactic approaches are ineffective.

Finally, and most significantly, demonstration role playing can produce a deeper understanding of the problem under discussion.

8

Training

Changes in human behavior frequently are the keys to increased organizational and interpersonal effectiveness. The problem-solving and decision-making capabilities of people are enhanced when they find new and better ways to utilize their own resources and draw on the resources of others. Training is the most provocative and challenging area in which role playing is utilized. Role playing facilitates changes in behavior. It is an action-learning method that produces both insight and skill in a wide range of situations for which merely giving information is an inadequate approach. Whenever well-established patterns of behavior need to be changed, information giving falls short of the goal. Bradford (1958) sums up contemporary thinking on this point:

> Let me offer one basic criterion we can use in testing any training or management development program. The fundamental goal of any program is to bring about a change in behavior. . . . We cannot be content with the assumption that learning information necessarily leads towards behavioral change in the way an individual actually performs back on the job. . . . Information and knowledge may lead to a shift in attitudes, but do not necessarily lead toward behavioral improvement.
>
> To take a tough-minded dollars-and-cents approach to management we cannot be content with less than improvement back on the job. (p. 4)

TRAINING OBJECTIVES

The basic objective of training is to change ineffective behavior or to maintain and reinforce effective behavior in order to achieve performance goals. Within this broad purpose three subgoals may be defined. The first of these is *training in methods*. A great many tasks require specific skills and techniques. Nurses, interviewers, fund raisers, teachers, sales representatives, and managers all use and develop systematic approaches to the problems they face. If operators in a factory must learn a step-by-step method to do a particular job, their supervisors must be taught job-training methods. In any training situation in which the emphasis is on teaching an established pattern of procedures, the approach is essentially *method centered.*

In addition, it is necessary in many training situations for participants to learn how to handle variations in problem situations. Thus the focus is on problems rather than on methods. The approach is *problem centered.*

Finally, the goal may be that trainees increase self-understanding. Such training deals with individual insight and personal effectiveness. The approach is *individual centered.*

In each of these three approaches, either of the two basic types of role playing can be used or combined. For example, in a session dealing with methods the facilitator may begin with a structured role play with written roles and observer sheets. Later the experience may become developmental in order to engage participants in defining their own goals and in developing procedures, structures, and techniques that go beyond the predetermined goals of the session.

Method-Centered Role Playing

A good example of method-centered training is provided by the Job Instruction Training (JIT) program developed by the War Manpower Commission during World War II. The program focused on teaching well-established techniques for training new employees. It was designed primarily for supervisors who were faced with the tremendous task of training the many marginal members of the labor market who entered defense industries during World War II. The goal of JIT was to provide supervisors with a step-by-step outline for instructing new employees. The four steps were: (a) prepare the worker, (b) present the operation, (c) try out performance, and (d) follow up. The JIT program comprised a series of demonstrations and lectures on how to accomplish these four steps, but the emphasis of the program was on developing effectiveness in *implementing* the process. The following is an example of a typical JIT role-play session.

> The role players are two members of a supervisory group, both of whom are being trained to instruct new employees. One supervisor plays the role of trainer and the other plays the role of a new worker. For purposes of illustration, the second step of the JIT process—present the operation—will be used.
>
> *Supervisor: All right, now that you know a little about the setup here and I've shown you how your work place is laid out, let's go over your job, step by step. Feel free to interrupt me at any time and to ask any questions that occur to you. I don't want you to worry if you don't get this the first time. We will just take our time and keep at it until I am able to make it clear. The first thing you do is pick up this housing and place it in this jig right in front of you. Is that clear?*
>
> *Employee: Yes.*

Supervisor: Now, with your right hand you pick up a bolt from this tray and at the same time with your left hand pick up a nut from the tray on your left. One thing to remember when you are picking up the bolt is always to pick it up by the head. This will save you time, you won't have to turn the bolt over in your hand, and it will be ready to insert in the housing. Place the bolt in the housing with your right hand, bring the nut up from below with your left, and tighten it finger-tight. Just two turns are needed.

The supervisor then continues to go through the job step by step, calling the worker's attention to key points that should be remembered. When the entire presentation of the operation has been made, the facilitator stops the action and solicits comments from the group.

Facilitator: In previous sessions we have discussed this job and broken it down; you each have a job breakdown that shows the steps and key points in carrying out the job. Do you have any comments on how this operation was presented to the worker?

Participant A: Yes, the supervisor left out a key point right at the start. The worker should have been told to place the housing with the flat surface in front. This is an important key point, because if the worker doesn't do it this way the housing will have to be turned around and that will waste time.

Facilitator (addressing the supervisor): How does that comment check out with your breakdown of how the job should be presented?

Supervisor: Yes, I'm afraid I left that key point out. I agree that it should be in the breakdown of the job.

Facilitator: Fine, you will notice that it takes almost a full second for the worker to turn the housing around if it is not placed properly to begin with, so you can see that when a worker is turning out four or five hundred of these pieces a day, one second per piece can amount to a lot of wasted time. I'm glad this came up because it shows how important a minor key point can be in helping the new worker get started correctly. Any other comments?

Participant B: Yes, I noticed that the instructor forgot to tell the employee that the first bolt should always be placed in the outer right-hand hole in the housing. If this isn't done there will be trouble further along in assembling the part.

This somewhat oversimplified illustration shows how a method-centered role-play approach can be utilized. Trainees are provided with an opportunity to try out their own effectiveness in instructing others and receive straightforward guidance based on a well-established pattern of job instruction. Successful training occurs when participants are able to go through an entire instruction situation covering all four basic steps in teaching the job in a systematic and clear way. This same approach is useful in teaching sales representatives key steps in presenting a product to a customer, in training nurses to follow established procedures in handling problems in patient care, and in dozens of other job-training situations.

Problem-Centered Role Playing

A Job Instruction Training situation also can be used to illustrate problem-centered training. Frequently job-instruction techniques are utilized in training experienced employees who have developed poor work habits or who are asked to change their methods of doing the job. In these situations, a step-by-step method of proceeding is not sufficient instruction. Straight JIT frequently does not "take" with experienced workers. Therefore, the supervisor not only must be trained in JIT methods, but also must develop understanding and insight concerning the experienced worker's feelings and attitudes. In the following example a group of supervisors are being trained in how to instruct experienced workers in a change in job methods.

After some warm-up and discussion a role-play situation is structured in which one group member plays the role of the supervisor and the second group member plays the role of an experienced worker. The person in the role of the worker may be briefed orally by the supervisor or a written briefing, which brings out key problems, may be prepared in advance by the facilitator.

Supervisor: Good morning, I would like to talk to you about something.

Employee: What's up?

Supervisor: First of all, you've been doing a fine job. We have a new method that I think is going to make your job easier and make it possible for you to get your job done with a little less effort. Let me show you how it works.

The supervisor then demonstrates the new technique.

Employee: Look, I've been doing this job for about six months, and I've gotten to the point where it's almost automatic with me. I turn out as much work as anyone else, and I'm really pretty satisfied with the way things are going.

Supervisor: Believe me, this is no criticism of you. I wouldn't be asking you to change your method if I were not sure that this new approach is really better.

Employee: Well, it may be better, but it took me a couple of months to catch on to this way of doing it and I had to work extra hard for a while in order to get my work out. If I change methods now it will mean going through that all over again. I can't see any advantage to that.

Here the supervisor is faced with a different problem from that in the first situation. Since the worker is resistant to the new procedure, the problem-centered approach is now appropriate. This involves giving the supervisory group members training in various ways of handling the conflict situation and in developing alternative courses of action. The focus of this session is on increasing the participants' understanding of the total situation and providing them with an opportunity to improve their skills in resolving such conflicts.

Obviously, this example can be generalized into many other areas. It is in some ways similar to the problem of the salesperson faced with the customer who is not ready to buy. It is not enough to tell a salesperson to smile, get the prospect's attention, talk briefly about something the prospect is interested in, talk benefits, and follow certain established procedures for closing the sale. The salesperson must learn to deal with dynamic situations and with a variety of people whose feelings and attitudes are paramount in determining the salesperson's effectiveness.

Interviewers can be taught to follow a pattern of questions, but the ability to perceive and understand the feelings of the interviewee, the ability to establish rapport and really listen provide a much greater challenge. An executive can be taught a great deal about planning, systems, controls, motivation theory, and so on. But in the executive role—perhaps more than in any other—the ability to administer and to adjust to change is most highly valued. Problem-centered role playing can be used to teach people to deal with these kinds of situations. Its major advantages are that it does not stereotype people or issues, that results are not predetermined, and that it is action training. It can be used in practically any situation in which a training group faces reasonably common problems that cannot be resolved with pat answers. If there is a best way to handle a situation, the training may consist of a lecture, written presentation, or method-centered role playing to demonstrate the best way. When the focus is on dealing with a complex social situation in which correct answers are not readily available, problem-centered role playing is most appropriate.

In problem-centered sessions, the role play should examine a general problem and not persons or personalities. This is not to say that individual insights are not developed in a problem-centered session. Certainly participants may increase their individual effectiveness and learn something new about their own personalities. The point is that the problem-centered session is primarily concerned with skills and processes and not with personality difficulties.

Individual-Centered Role Playing

A Job Instruction Training situation again will be used to illustrate individual-centered role playing, which deals with an individual's personal problems in handling a specific situation. An office supervisor has an unusually high rate of turnover in her department. Investigation discloses that her subordinates are poorly trained and have negative attitudes about their supervisor and the company. Termination interviews reveal that employees feel that the supervisor is curt and tactless. In a role-play session, role reversal and the mirror technique are used to increase the supervisor's awareness of the effect of her behavior on others. As her awareness increases, she is encouraged to experiment with new approaches.

Integration of Role-Play Approaches

Method-centered, problem-centered and individual-centered role-play approaches all can be used in a given session. Although the facilitator may begin the session on a method-centered basis, it may become clear that although trainees can follow step-by-step procedures quite closely, they are unable to handle situations that depart from the established pattern. In this situation it is effective for the facilitator to switch to a more experimental method in which various approaches are tested and evaluated with emphasis on developing flexibility and sensitivity in handling the problem. Group members may discover personal and attitudinal blocks that must be dealt with before either methods or skills can be developed. An effective facilitator will deal with whatever is present in the situation, that is, with the "here and now."

The previous discussion shows that role playing can be applied to a wide range of situations. There are two rather broad areas in which role playing is particularly suitable. The first is human relations training, the second, management and executive training. Because of the almost universal use of role playing in human relations training and its peculiar suitability for executive training, these two areas will be considered in detail.

HUMAN RELATIONS TRAINING

The use of the term human relations to describe a particular training area is somewhat misleading, for human relations are involved in almost every training situation. Nevertheless, in many training programs a series of sessions are devoted specifically to human relations principles and skills. Role playing brings an impact and intensity to these sessions that rarely can be duplicated by other techniques. Its use in human relations sessions fits into three general categories: (a) training in human relations principles, (b) training in human relations skills, and (c) training in self-awareness.

Training in Human Relations Principles

An intellectual understanding of human relations can be communicated through lectures and other information-giving techniques. Role playing, however, can be used to change, or at least lay the foundation for changing, attitudes. Thus role playing can transform a purely instructional session into a more significant learning experience in which the trainee becomes deeply involved. For example, a facilitator may lecture on the principle that behavior is caused, explaining the stimulus-response idea, frustration-aggression hypothesis, or other theoretical material. But a role play could illustrate these principles and produce involvement on the part of the participants. In this case, rather than merely communicate information, the facilitator could provide an opportunity for exposure of attitudes and behavior and for feedback of reactions.

In the following example a training group is informed that it is about to witness an interview between a supervisor and a subordinate and a second interview with a staff person. The supervisor is to ask the subordinate to work overtime. The group is asked to watch the behavior of the supervisor and the subordinate. In the second interview, a staff associate who works for the personnel department will be asked to stay late to be available to the employees who are working overtime. The training group is told to look for differences in the way the subordinates act and to try to decide why these differences exist. The group also is to watch the supervisor to see if his or her reactions seem to change in each of the interviews and, if so, why. (The facilitator can supply the group members with observer sheets on which to identify their reactions.)

Each role player is given a written role that provides background information and a point of view on the problem. The persons playing the roles of subordinate and personnel representative are asked to leave the room and to re-enter separately so that they are not influenced by the other's interview.

The roles supplied to the players can be as complicated as the facilitator feels is necessary; however, for purposes of this illustration, the roles are fairly simple and brief.

Bill Jones, Production Supervisor: You are fifty years old, and you have been with this company for twenty-seven years. Your boss just told you that a rush order has come in and you will have to stay tonight and get it out. It will be necessary for you to ask some of your subordinates to work overtime. You have called one of them; he is on his way to your office now. You also are going to ask the Equal Employment Opportunities (EEO) coordinator from the personnel department to stay. Since several of your operators have complained about unequal treatment regarding overtime and job assignments, you expect some problems tonight, and you would like to have the EEO coordinator present.

One of the things that annoys you about this situation is that there have been three rush orders in the last ten days. As far as you are concerned, this is a result of poor planning on the part of the production control department. You had made plans to play bridge with friends tonight, so you know your wife is going to be annoyed. You will have to call and tell her you won't be home.

Another thing that bothers you is that you know your people are not going to like this, or at least some of them won't. They like the money that comes from working overtime, but they like to know enough in advance so that they can make plans. You know, too, that several people are unhappy about their assignments.

Because you are a foreman you don't get paid for the overtime at all; your subordinates are really getting a much better break than you are. Actually, the operators' overtime plus their base wages will bring their pay almost up to yours. You have the responsibility for the whole department and you work more hours than anyone in it, but the pay differential is pretty small. Nevertheless, there are still some advantages in being the boss.

Sam Goode, Operator: You feel that management is doing a poor job of planning. One week they don't have enough work, the next week they have too much. They also keep shifting your assignments around. You have been here quite a while, and you feel that you need to make it clear that you won't be pushed around.

Phyllis Streeter, Equal Employment Opportunities Coordinator: You just joined this company after several years of conducting programs for minority groups and women for a large voluntary agency. You feel that many managers in this present organization want to use you as a crutch. They ask you to sit in on performance reviews, come in on late shifts to handle complaints, and generally serve as a troubleshooter. You have been directed by your boss not to get trapped into doing the managers' jobs. Your assignment is to set up equal-opportunities programs, train managers in EEO guidelines, and investigate and resolve complaints. You are not expected to take over the manager's basic job, which is to assign work equitably, stay within EEO guidelines, and aid his or her own people effectively.

After setting the climate of the role play for the group and the individual players, the facilitator directs that the two interviews be conducted. They are limited to about five minutes each and are uninterrupted.

Upon completion of the interviews, the facilitator guides the group in a discussion and analysis. Group members are asked to comment on differences in the way the two players responded to the supervisor. As these differences are noted and discussed, the facilitator can encourage the group to analyze why the differences existed. The group's reactions can be checked with the players. For example, the group might agree that the two players were treated differently. The facilitator can then ask the person who played the manager whether this was true.

Facilitator: Do you think that you treated the EEO coordinator differently from the worker?

Manager: Yes, because she was not reporting to me.

Facilitator: How did that affect you?

Manager: Well, when I began to feel that she wasn't on my side, I decided I had better be careful.

The group members then discuss whether this explains the manager's behavior and they look for other causes for his reaction. Gradually they may clarify the idea that power, authority, and trust are factors that cause different responses.

The facilitator can assist the group members in generalizing the results of their observations and discussion. As tentative conclusions are drawn, they can be tied in with specific incidents that occurred during the role playing. By the time the session ends, the group members are almost sure to agree that the behavior and responses of subordinates are caused by a variety of factors, such as the personality and temperament of the individual, his or her past experiences with supervisors, and the forces and pressures acting on each person at the time the interview occurs.

Thus, although a lecture could be used to teach supervisors about this particular aspect of human relations, a role play can bring drama and involvement to the learning situation. A theoretical concept can, in this way, take on real meaning and provide the basis for subsequent changes in attitude and behavior.

Training in Human Relations Skills

An increasing number of facilitators have been attracted to the idea of teaching human relations skills. The ability to motivate people, resolve conflicts, and handle a variety of interpersonal problems is, at least to some extent, dependent on the development and utilization of basic social skills. Role playing well suits such training. A few examples follow.

SETTING GOALS

Background

In most organizations, supervisors and managers are specifically charged with responsibility for working with subordinates to plan for improved performance. In some organizations management by objectives (MBO) systems are used. In others there are less formal methods for ensuring that managers inform their subordinates as to what is expected or work with them to establish performance criteria and specific performance goals. The interpersonal and human relations skills required in these situations include:

1. Giving straightforward information to subordinates without humiliating or embarrassing them or diminishing their involvement and commitment.
2. Developing a two-way flow of information so that goals can be set with mutual understanding and commitment.

Learning to do these things becomes the goal for this session.

Instructions (for the facilitator)

1. Select a group member to role play a manager and give the "manager" information about the subordinate's areas of responsibility and a specific goal concern (e.g., the subordinate is responsible for recruiting new people and there are too many positions open).
2. Select a member to be the subordinate and give that person similar information about the situation.
3. Make sure that each of the role players is given a slightly different point of view based on slightly different information. For example, the manager's role should include the idea that more time should be spent on recruitment and selection. The subordinate's role should point out that there are a great many demands on his or her time and that allocation of additional time for recruitment and selection would reduce effectiveness in other areas. The roles also should contain differences in priorities in terms of costs and allocation of other human resources.
4. An observer (or observers) is provided with a check list that includes items such as:

      a. What did the manager do in order to maintain a two-way flow of information?

      b. Did the manager present information clearly without premature value judgments, pressure, or equivocation?

Note: The person playing the part of the manager then begins to interact with the individual in the subordinate's role. Differences of opinion gradually surface. The purpose of the activity should be made clear at the beginning: the manager and subordinate are concerned with developing goals that each feels are appropriate and that can be used as a basis for judging performance in the future. The observer provides feedback on the degree to which the manager has used human relations techniques that have been presented or discussed prior to the role play. The observer also may give feedback to the subordinate (e.g., in what ways did the subordinate create tension? In what ways might he or she have presented a point of view without hostility or defensiveness while still maintaining an opportunity for a two-way flow of influence?).

MOTIVATING VOLUNTARY WORKERS

Background

      In a nonprofit, volunteer organization there is a need to obtain the cooperation and involvement of large numbers of nonpaid volunteers. Those concerned with involving volunteers need to develop skill in communicating effectively so that the volunteers' motivations and interests are tapped and they feel a part of the agency and have a desire to follow through in the mission of the agency.

Instructions (for the facilitator)

   1. Describe and demonstrate the basic techniques for engaging volunteer workers. List the basic steps in the process, for example:

      a. Be sure the volunteer understands the mission of the agency.

      b. Provide an opportunity for the volunteer to raise objections or questions regarding the task to which he or she is assigned.

      c. Use developmental techniques to encourage the volunteer to understand and become involved in the agency's mission.

   (A more detailed definition of techniques or demonstrations on film or videotape can be presented.)

   2. In order to facilitate the training process, ask group members (managers or team captains in a volunteer agency) to identify from their own past experiences a specific person (who remains anonymous) who was resistant to an assignment. Have each person write a very brief description of the nature of that resistance on the recording sheet provided.

   3. Divide the members into subgroups for multiple role playing (two to four people in each subgroup).

   4. Select one person in each subgroup to play the role of the resistant person whom he or she has identified. This brings authenticity to the case.

   5. Select a second member of each group to play the part of the manager and to attempt to understand the nature of the resistance in order to cope with it.

   6. Another member of each subgroup later can be asked to play the role of the resistant client while a second member takes on the managerial role.

7. Throughout these enactments observer guides and observer feedback are utilized. Thus, people acquire firsthand experience in dealing with resistance, have a chance to practice the skills and techniques that were discussed earlier in the session,and have an opportunity to share ideas based on their own experiences.

General human relations skills such as listening, dealing with conflict, providing direction, and leading group discussions can be explored and improved through role playing. Specific organization-based techniques also can be practiced and improved through this method. For example, many organizations use fairly standardized interviewing techniques for personnel selection, counseling, or sales interviews. Skill practice often is needed to ensure that these procedures are understood and that they are responded to realistically and with sensitivity and awareness. Often these sessions can be strengthened by the use of audiovisual supporting devices (Shaw, 1967). Individuals can be tape recorded while conducting interviews, and the tapes can be played back and critiqued in small-group sessions. Illustrations or desirable models can be presented on film or tape; techniques, procedures, and strategies also can be presented in taped or written form. It often is useful to provide "living case studies" through film or videotape to evoke a higher level of interest and involvement. However, all these methods are supplemental to the basic process of providing skill practice through action learning. This is the core of the role-play process. Regardless of the nature of the subject matter, the presentations, the observer techniques, and the use of media, the strength of the process lies in the fact that people are actively trying out new behavior and obtaining experience in applying what they know or what has been presented for exploration and application.

Training in Self-Awareness

Human relations skills are often treated mechanically; the learner finds that he or she is following "good" human relations practices but somehow is not quite getting across as he or she wishes. A great many human relations and communications problems are caused by lack of clarity on the part of the individual regarding personal feelings, goals, and potential. There are two basic processes for enhancing self-awareness and utilizing and building one's own potential: feedback and learning through action.

Feedback. The idea that people learn through experience is part of most learning theory. However, experience alone often is not enough to create self-awareness. It is possible to experience a situation dozens of times without ever being aware of one's own impact or limitations. Thus, a salesperson may make dozens of calls without ever being aware of the alienating characteristic of being too pushy or aggressive. A manager may not be aware that absorption in technical and managerial problems creates the feeling in others that he or she is aloof or disinterested.

Until one receives feedback there is a strong possibility that one's behavior patterns will not change. Self-awareness is enhanced by constructive feedback. Role playing provides a focus of action in which feedback can be given.

Example: A company president participated in a computer simulation in which he and his associates played the roles of key executives in a hypothetical company. Their team was in competition with similar company teams using the same computer-based case situation. Each team made decisions that affected its own "profitability and effectiveness" as well as competing teams. In the process of playing his role in this situation, the president took over, dominated the group, and was not receptive to input from others. His team failed in its efforts to develop profits (in fact, the team went bankrupt during the simulation). During feedback sessions following the role play, the president learned that members of his team had felt oppressed and uninvolved because of his dominance. Through this feedback the president began experimenting with new ways of running the hypothetical organization and carried back some of these insights to his own company.

Example: A group of administrators from the same public school system participated in a training session on communication skills. One of the objectives of the session was to enhance self-awareness. Each of the school administrators participated in a variety of role-play exercises in giving instructions, coaching and counseling teachers, and increasing assertiveness and responsiveness. Several members of the group—through the feedback received during the activities and the summary of feedback made toward the end of the session—became aware that in their desire to be "nice" they had withheld some of their own insights and, in many instances, had covered up their own desire to have impact. In the process of covering up (and acting in a wishy-washy or nonassertive manner) they nevertheless had been perceived as being slightly hostile or defensive. One administrator summed up her reactions to and insights based on the role play and feedback as follows:

> I thought I was covering up some of my own anxieties and that I was winning people over by being a nice, cooperative person. I now realize that it is more useful to be straightforward without being abrasive, and I plan to stop being so apologetic and self-effacing when I am dealing with colleagues and students.

Learning Through Action. The idea that one can change through experience has been stressed throughout discussions of role-play methods. One dimension of that learning is that the individual role player can become more aware of his or her own feelings, an awareness that, in turn, will lead to more effective action. Specialized applications of role playing such as behavior rehearsal, behavior modeling, and various forms of assertiveness training provide opportunities for identifying one's own resources. In behavior rehearsal, for example, an individual is asked to repeat a response to a given situation several times until the feelings associated with that situation become more clear and the individual is more in touch with those feelings. In assertiveness training individuals are often asked to state a specific goal in regard to an interaction they are about to have; e.g., "I want to be more forceful," or "I want to be more clear and precise," or "I want to avoid appearing apologetic or self-demeaning." By practicing a more affirmative or assertive series of statements in a role play, the individual can increase his or her capacity to use resources that may not have been tapped in the past. Role playing can be used to develop increased awareness and the capacity to utilize one's resources more effectively.

STATING STRENGTHS

Background

In a small group it may become clear that quite a few of the members are nonassertive and rarely seem able to act decisively or with conviction. Each member can be asked to participate in a brief role play.

Instructions (for the facilitator)

1. Announce that each member of the group is being considered for increased responsibility or a promotion and that a personnel-selection committee has instructed each member to do the following: "Tell us all your strengths, good points, and positive resources. Don't hold back. Feel free to be egotistical, to brag about yourself, even to exaggerate some of your strengths."
2. Wait a few seconds and then announce that each member is to imagine that he or she is about to meet that committee to present his or her strengths and resources as forcefully and positively as possible.
3. Direct each member, in turn, to take on the role. Instruct other group members to ask for more information or to comment if the role-playing individual is apologetic, negative, or self-demeaning during the process.

STATING OPINIONS

Background

During a session with a group of first-level supervisors it often becomes clear that many of them feel that they are unable to oppose their manager(s) when they think that they are right and he or she is wrong. After some role playing and discussion it becomes clear that even when the supervisors feel strongly about something, many of them express their views tentatively and apologetically. The following role play is conducted to increase effectiveness and self-awareness.

Instructions (for the facilitator)

1. Announce that each group member is to think of a fairly recent situation in which he or she was trying to convince the boss of a given objective and was not successful in winning the argument. Say that each person will play his or her own role and is to use some techniques and devices for strengthening his or her approach. Stress that although this may not be the way each

member would want to handle the problem in real life, the objective of the activity is to become clearer about one's own convictions and resources in presenting new ideas. Say that each individual is to state his or her idea positively, point out its benefits, and say why it will work.

2. Distribute paper and pencils and tell each member to write down one or two sentences that summarize the positive convictions that the member has about his or her idea.

3. When everyone is ready, select one individual who will face another individual in the group and present his or her idea. Say that the second individual should not resist, argue, or comment, but should simply listen.

4. Instruct observers to tell each participant if he or she apologizes, appears overly tentative, does not speak loudly or firmly, or fails to express his or her conviction with clarity and strength.

5. Ask each member, in turn, to repeat the activity until the observers are convinced that the participant has expressed the idea with conviction and strength.

6. All members of the group then discuss the activity. In what ways could the presentations have been stronger, more firm, or more affirmative? Were they loud enough? Was there positive eye contact? Was conviction communicated? What other points have the members learned from the experience?

Note: Regardless of feedback, each individual should repeat his or her conviction, changing words or phrases that could be improved but not extending the presentation beyond two or three sentences. This is repeated with other members of the group until everyone agrees that the presentation is being made with appropriate force and assertion.

MANAGEMENT AND EXECUTIVE TRAINING

Thousands of top executives and, in fact, several presidents of the United States have used role playing to deepen their understanding of a wide range of management and communication issues. Presidents role play press conferences with a staff member, obtain feedback, revise their presentations, and try again. Top executives in marketing organizations often are asked to play large purchasers or customers to "get a feel" for a marketing or public-relations issue. Reviewing performance, engaging others in decision-making processes, and responding to and managing conflict are all areas in which role playing is being used for skill development, not only among supervisors but also in the highest echelons of public agencies, educational systems, and business and industry.

Trends in Management Education

"Within the last two decades . . . management has carried on its own revolution—a revolution of self-improvement" (Redfield, 1953, p. 1). Awareness that management is a skilled profession with its own body of knowledge has grown at an increased tempo in recent years. The problem of defining executive training needs and objectives has attracted the attention of many observers of the management scene.

Roethlisberger (1951) clarified the educational needs of executives:

> What industry and business must have in their supervisory and administrative groups is more educated people . . . not more trained seals. . . . By an "educated person" I mean a person (1) who knows what he does not know; (2) who has an honest perplexity and curiosity about his personal experiences; (3) who has a stop, look, and listen attitude toward his own experience and is capable of re-evaluating and learning from it; and (4) who has some skills in the direction of being able to receive communication from others. (p. 50)

Murray (1958) identified executives' needs in this way:

> . . . the leader must have perceptiveness, insight, and know-how at a much higher level. He must be much more of a scientist. He must be an artist and a philosopher as well. (p. 2)

Appley (1956) focused on the intangible needs of the manager when he said:

> An enlightened manager is an artist. He is highly skilled in individual effectiveness with people. (p. 6)

And Cleveland (1972), with firsthand experience as an executive in both the private and public sector, commented on the changing requirements for leaders in increasingly complex organizations:

> The management of large organization systems will require a great deal of talking and listening in an effort to take every interest into account and yet emerge with relevant policy decisions and executive action. The world's work will not be tackled by identifying our differences, but by sitting down, preferably at a round table, working hard at the politics of consensus, bringing people together rather than splitting them apart. (p. 84)

These comments reflect a comparatively recent trend in management education: a trend toward concern with social skills—the ability to relate effectively to other people, to be more aware of one's own behavior and its effect on others.

The era of Taylor (1948) and Gilbreth (1911) left its stamp on management in the form of a more scientific and systematic approach to problems of administration. Automation, operations research, linear programing, and other scientific techniques are the modern-day counterparts of the original systems and methods work that scientific management practitioners originated. Almost simultaneously the work of Mayo (1933) and Roethlisberger and Dixon (1939) established the foundation for a humanistic movement in industry. It has been the basis for an expanding concern with the interpersonal and human relations skills of executives.

A Paradox

The current trend in management thinking and education presents some paradoxical problems for the training facilitator. Until now the facilitator has been concerned primarily with selling the need for human relations training and the development of social skills. Now students are aware of this need, and in many instances executives can speak with authority and erudition about human relations principles and theories. They no longer want to know "what" or "why," but "how." Role playing is essentially a "how to" technique. Its training potential cannot be duplicated by other methods. The greatest single value of role playing in executive training is that it can be utilized as a "how to" technique for developing social skills.

Application

The application of role playing in executive training programs presents very few special problems. The same basic techniques used in human relations training are suitable. In fact, the increasing awareness among executives concerning their need for improved social skills often makes role playing particularly appealing to them.

When structured role-play cases are used, the content must, of course, be suitable to an executive group. This does not require changing the basic issues involved, merely dressing those issues in new clothing. For example, earlier in this chapter a case was used as an example of human relations training. The case involved a manager, a subordinate, and a personnel representative. The manager wanted the subordinate to respond to a particular need, i.e., to agree to work overtime to fill a special order. The case was used to increase the participants' understanding of situational causes of behavior. The roles can be adapted for use with an executive group as follows.

Harry Olsen, Executive Vice President: You are the chief operating executive of this company and report directly to the president and chairman of the board. About a year ago, you recommended that an expansion program that had been underway for several years should be curtailed. The board, however, voted to continue the program. Yesterday the president called you in and told you that company costs must be reduced by 10 percent. You feel that if the board had acted on your original suggestion this drastic cut in costs would not be necessary. You know that most of your division executives are not going to like this move even if it is about time that they came back down to earth.

Susan Miller, Vice President, Purchasing: You were recently promoted to your present job and now report to Harry Olsen, the executive vice president. You have heard rumblings about a new push to cut costs. You have been getting ready to recommend the purchase of about $25,000 worth of new equipment. You know that the equipment will pay for itself in about six years and it has a "life" of about twelve years. It would reduce some production headaches, and you would still like to purchase it. Nevertheless, you are new on this job and you don't know your boss too well. You think perhaps you should build his confidence in you before you argue for something you can get along without.

By experiencing the case and exploring the impact of each player's behavior on the other participants, the group can increase its awareness of the dynamics of interpersonal communication and the impact of past experience on current behavior.

SUMMARY

Role playing is applicable in a great many training situations. It is useful in methods training, problem solving, and increasing personal effectiveness. There are three basic training approaches:

1. Method-centered role playing is intended to teach specific methods and techniques. The emphasis is on *procedure* rather than on attitudes, feelings, or random forces that could affect the implementation of the procedure.
2. Problem-centered role playing is designed to increase the participant's ability to handle specific problem situations. The focus is on common problems. Rather than dealing with step-by-step methods, the training is designed to deal with the task of increasing understanding and changing attitudes. Although the role plays focus on specific problems, they are designed so that broad standards of behavior and performance can be generalized.
3. Individual-centered role playing is used to deal with the individual's personal problems in handling difficult situations. Although common supervisory problems may be dealt with, the focus tends to be on the individual's personal blocks and attitudes.

Human relations training and executive training are two of the most challenging areas in which role playing can be applied. Human relations training is concerned with how to relate and respond to people. Management training is concerned with how to develop the ability to achieve results through individuals and groups. Role playing is a most useful "how to" training technique.

REFERENCES

Appley, L. A. An enlightened manager. *Management News*, 1956, 29(6).

Bradford, L. P. A look at management growth and development. *Journal of the American Society of Training Directors*, 1958, 12(7), 4.

Cleveland, H. *The future executive*. New York: Harper & Row, 1972.

Gilbreth, F. B. *Motion study.* New York: D. Van Nostrand, 1911.

Mayo, G. E. *The human problems of American industrial civilization.* Boston, MA: Harvard Business School, 1933.

Murray, E. How an educator looks at industrial activities in the field of communication. *Journal of Communication*, 1958, 6(2).

Redfield, C. E. *Communication in management.* Chicago: The University of Chicago Press, 1953.

Roethlisberger, F. J. Training supervisors in human relations. *Harvard Business Review*, 1951, 29(5), 50.

Roethlisberger, F. J., & Dixon, W. J. *Management and the worker.* Cambridge, MA: Harvard University Press, 1939.

Shaw, M. Television in management development: Pros and cons of a rapidly-growing training method. *Training and Development Journal*, February, 1967,

Taylor, F. W. *Scientific management.* New York: Harper & Row, 1948.

9

Evaluating

All human behavior can be considered as the testing of hypotheses. A person who jumps over a puddle is testing the hypothesis that he has judged the size of the puddle correctly and has evaluated his jumping capacity adequately. A person who consistently does not (or cannot) evaluate himself and his surroundings accurately probably will not survive long in an environment that contains many hazards.

In working life many judgments are required for success. The ability to "size up" one's peers, subordinates, and supervisors is an advantage. Particularly in the area of personnel selection, the ability to make an appropriate decision can be crucial.

Many situations, however, call for a judgment when there is almost no basis for making an adequate decision. Ordinarily, a general rule is that the more information one has, the better the decision. In addition, the more pertinent the information the better.

Sources of information can be diverse: one can use historical data, interview data, test data, and observational data. All are valuable, but for decisions that have to do with human relations skills, such as the selection of a supervisor, the best kind of information is observation. Actually seeing how the person does in various situations is more important than hearsay evidence (testimonials, letters of recommendation) or secondary evidence (tests, interviews, and impressions).

Another selection tool is the psychological test. This type of test can be divided into two general categories, standardized and projective.

STANDARDIZED TESTS

Standardized test procedures are rigorously established by the test constructor; the examiner must use the test as a laboratory instrument in the exact procedure specified in the manual. The subject is restricted; only specific things will result in a good score. The completed test is scored mechanically, and raw scores are transmuted into interpretable sources such as percentiles and ratings.

If a person achieves a rating of "A" on the Strong Interest Test for the salesperson variable, it is interpreted that the subject's interests are similar to those of others in sales and, thus, the subject may be a good bet as a salesperson. If a child evidences an IQ of 125 on the Stanford Binet Test, superior intelligence is indicated and the child may be expected to do well scholastically.

A standardized test is standardized not only in terms of administration and scoring; it is also standardized in terms of interpretation. If the test is suitably administered to people to whom it is applicable, the final product—the score—is rigorously interpreted.

PROJECTIVE TESTS

A projective test is very different from a standardized test in that the examiner is all-important. The examiner does not follow specific instructions and is not limited to single dimensions of interpretation. Both the subject and the examiner have much more freedom.

For example, the Rorschach test—the best known and most studied of the projective tests—consists of ink blots to which subjects respond in terms of what they see. Subjects are not asked to answer specific questions; they are free to respond with anything that comes to mind. The examiner listens to the responses, records them, and later analyzes them, and—on the basis of his or her judgment of the meaning of the responses, considering up to one hundred different variables such as the location of the perception, how it was seen, its content, the reaction times, the approach to the cards, and so forth—comes to a variety of conclusions about the individual's personality factors, including such items as drive, intelligence, types of interest, nature of personal problems, and psychiatric diagnoses. While almost all examiners will come to more or less the same conclusions using standardized tests, there will be considerably more variation from the use of projective techniques.

Role playing, like the Rorschach, is a projective technique. Different observers may see different things and may interpret them in different ways. The subject, as in the case of the Rorschach, can vary his or her responses to the stimuli made by the antagonists. What the subject says and how it is said gives the observer insight into how the subject reacts to life and what kind of person the subject is.

ROLE PLAYING FOR TESTING

The validity of a test depends on the agreement between the interpretation of the test and the reality it is supposed to measure. If someone creates a new test and calls it a test of intelligence, to validate it the creator must prove that it really does measure intelligence. This can be done in a number of ways. For example, the test can be correlated with other tests of intelligence; scores of children of varying ages can be compared; or the test can be used in a clinical fashion to see if predictions work out for individuals.

The validity of role playing as a test depends on the degree of reality measurement that takes place: whether the individual performing on the stage bears any resemblance to the individual in real life or whether the artificial situation and the contrived problem elicit behavior that is typical of the individual. The question is crucial. There is some evidence that role playing is a good procedure for understanding others.

Clinical Judgments

Role playing has been used by many psychologists who know their patients rather well and who have found that in the playing of roles people tend to become themselves. In the stress of having to deal with antagonists rapidly, people are unable to act in any way but their usual manner. After exciting sessions in which there is a good deal of give and take, subjects often report that the situation seemed very realistic.

Experimental Evidence

Borgatta (1956) conducted a classical experiment to investigate the relationship between actual natural behavior, role-playing behavior, and test results. He found that real behavior could be predicted better from role playing than from psychological tests.

Logical Evidence

A function is the best measure of itself. If one wishes to know if a person can type, the best way to find out is to have the person type, rather than to try to determine this by an interview, school ratings, or other processes. So, too, if one is interested in determining what a person's behavior is in complex situations in which the person has to interact with other people, it seems evident that a test situation of exactly that type is best.

We make judgments about people from how they look, how they act, and how they talk. The snap impressions that we make about others, although they may be wrong in some cases, probably have a good deal of general validity. The interview is an example. When a job is open the interviewer has some concept in mind of the kind of person needed in terms of personality, character, and ability. A good interviewer will be able to size up each individual rapidly, coming to conclusions on the basis of many impressions of the individual. Research on interviews indicates that people form rather definite impressions of others on the basis of very little information.

In considering methods for the evaluation of people, there are at least four considerations to keep in mind: (a) the purpose of the evaluation, (b) who is being evaluated, (c) who is evaluating, and (d) necessary validity. The following are some examples:

1. A child of six is brought to a school, and the principal wants to determine whether the child is ready for the first grade. Probably the best procedure would be to call in a school psychologist to give the child reading readiness and scholastic achievement tests.
2. An employer wishes to know whether an applicant is a competent truck driver. He will probably ask the applicant to get into a truck and drive it.
3. A young woman applies for a position as a junior executive. She is just out of college and has no work experience. In this case, role playing would be a way to test her for certain skills and characteristics.

In some cases none of these procedures may be effective. The child may be disturbed by the testing experience and do poorly. The truck driver may have skill but be unreliable. The junior executive may do poorly in a role play but still have good potential. No test is perfect. But everything considered, the best test of a function is the function itself. To the degree that the testing procedures are realistic, they are valid.

Role playing is the theoretically preferred procedure for the evaluation of complex interactive abilities—where individuals have to think and deal with one or more other persons and where emotional, intellectual, and behavioral elements occur simultaneously or in close succession. To test elements separately and then attempt to synthesize them is dangerous; a person is not merely the sum of his or her parts.

We can approach this subject from a different angle. An individual who is interviewed for a particular job and told that he is not satisfactory may be convinced that he can do the job and that those who are judging him are wrong in their opinions. Based on his training, willingness, and experience he may simply say, "Give me a chance." The logic is obvious; surely the best way to know whether the person will succeed is to try him out. If role playing is a test of itself, if a person plays a role as he would play it in real life, then role playing is a way to give somebody a chance to try out. The purpose of role playing for testing is to see how people interact with others in specific situations. Just as it makes sense to evaluate an applicant who wants to sing by having the person sing, so too it makes sense to evaluate a person who is applying for a job that involves dealing with others with a procedure that involves dealing with others.

Role playing for testing creates a realistic situation in which the individual operates holistically and dynamically. In a short space of time, observers can form conclusions about the individual's methods, skills, and characteristics.

Purposes

Role playing for testing has two general purposes: *evaluation* and *analysis*. Both are variations of the same general purpose: *understanding*.

Evaluation. Evaluation means classification. An individual who has been tested is given a label. Usually the label is part of a series that covers the entire spectrum of

valuation. For example, the labeling may be dichotomous, such as "acceptable—not acceptable," or it may be categorical, such as "A, B, C, D" with various
connotations. In military physical examinations, people are graded according to
classes of physical fitness.

Example: The president of a small firm that sells restaurant products had
considerable difficulty finding suitable salespeople. Interviewing, checking references, training the salespeople, and having them go out with more experienced
salespeople was expensive, and the rate of attrition from resignation or unsatisfactory performance was too high. Only one good salesperson was found out of
every seven hired, and only one was hired out of every seven interviewed.

Role playing was offered as a solution to the selection problem. All candidates
were invited to a hotel conference room, where the company president explained
the difficulty the company had experienced. Applicants were told that instead of
filling out questionnaires, having their references checked, and being interviewed,
they would be evaluated in on-the-job situations. Each person was told to enter the
testing room carrying a suitcase of samples. Each applicant was given a sheet
containing a description of the product. In the testing room each applicant was told
to make, successively, three presentations to three different people.

In the testing rooms, three veteran salespeople served as customers. One
handled the applicant in a friendly manner, another in a rough manner, and the
third in a hesitating manner. The "customers" were told to purchase material if
they felt like it. Each applicant came in separately and did not see or hear the other
presentations. After each presentation, the veterans (examiners) wrote their judgments of the applicant's abilities.

Ten potential salespeople were tested in the morning and ten more in the
afternoon. This procedure was repeated one day a month for four months. The
average of one successful selection out of seven increased to one out of three. The
president of the firm, calculating expenses alone, said that costs had dropped
one-half while success in selection had improved over 100 percent. The value of
this procedure was that the applicants were tested "at work" in different situations
by experts who could see how the applicants conducted themselves with different,
but typical, restaurant owners and managers. They were, in a sense, tried out in
realistic situations. From the point of view of the applicants, less time was wasted
in evaluation, and they received some insight about their performances.

Another example of role playing for evaluation illustrates how this procedure
can be used in real-life situations without special equipment or special assistants.
The position of receptionist was opened in a large office, and the other employees
were informed that they could apply for this job, which had higher prestige and a
higher salary than typing and clerking positions. All applicants were generally
familiar with the work of the receptionist. At the end of one work day, the
personnel officer took the applicants one at a time, asked them to sit behind the
receptionist's desk, and then played the roles of a number of people who might
come to the receptionist with various queries and for a number of purposes. Each

applicant was independently tested by the personnel officer, who served not only as the director, but also as the visitor and the observer.

One applicant, who never would have been considered for the job because she had been in the office a relatively short time, did the most outstanding job of playing the role of receptionist. She showed wit, sparkle, and aplomb. She was hired and proved to be entirely satisfactory.

Analysis. Analysis means the evaluation of subparts, the comparative ratings of parts, the comprehension of the meaning of isolated elements. Analysis in role playing is usually done for the purpose of understanding the strong and weak points of an individual or as a process to eliminate the weak parts and strengthen the good parts. In considering role playing for analysis we enter a more complex area; we are no longer dealing with a simple, overall decision but rather with the examination and evaluation of many elements in dynamic functioning.

Example: An engineer had been made the works manager of a firm, supplanting a retired employee who had been considered outstandingly successful. The engineer had more than seven years of experience in the firm, was well trained, was considered a hard worker, was respected by his fellow engineers for his technical competence, and was regarded as a mover. However, he turned out to be a complete failure in his new position. He seemed to antagonize everyone. Personnel turnover rates went up, production dropped, and morale was visibly reduced. Despite the fact that he was regarded as an outstanding engineer, he seemed to be a very poor administrator although no one quite knew what was wrong with him. At the insistence of his own supervisor—the president of the firm—he enrolled in a course designed to develop leaders.

The engineer role played a number of typical situations before observers, other supervisors who kept notes and then explained to him in detail what they thought he did wrong. Entirely concerned with efficiency, he was merciless in criticizing people who made mistakes, condemning them to too great an extent. He did not really listen to others, had little interest in their ideas, and wanted to have his own way. The entire group of managers explained, in great detail, a number of human relations errors that he made. One by one these errors were discussed, and one by one he refused to accept them as errors. He admitted his behavior and defended it. He refused to change his approach, and instead he attacked high and low—the officials for not backing him, his subordinates for their laxness, stupidity, and stubbornness. After the diagnosis, he left the course, convinced that it could do him no good.

This individual's problem was diagnosed, but he refused treatment. The engineer-turned-works-manager had a particular view of life and refused to change it. We may say that his attitude was foolish, since he might have been a success had he learned some human relations skills; or we may say that his attitude was commendable, showing his independence in his refusal to adjust to the opinions of others. In any case, he refused to accept the implications of the analysis: that he needed to change.

Another case will illustrate a successful use of analysis and the employment of a procedure for intensive analysis. A school principal who had been recently appointed to the position found that she was having a difficult time in supervising teachers. On role playing some typical situations she showed some characteristics that were rated as unsatisfactory. She was told that she displayed, for example, a sense of superiority. She answered, "Well, I am supposed to know all the answers, aren't I?" She was criticized for her curtness and abruptness and she answered: "I am not working to become popular." On being criticized for arbitrary behavior, she answered, "I have to make decisions. That's my job." As frequently happens in analysis, the individual felt threatened and defended herself. However, in this case the principal ultimately accepted the feedback and made an effort to improve her interpersonal effectiveness. The necessary step between diagnosis and training is acceptance of the validity of the criticism. How this is accomplished sometimes is a crucial problem.

The role-play facilitator made a check list of the principal's errors by asking the observers to write sentences commenting on the mistakes they felt she made. These errors were then tabulated and posted. Similar ideas were condensed. Eighteen errors were located, and the facilitator asked the observers to vote on whether or not they felt that the principal had made the particular errors. They were asked to vote "true" if they thought they had seen her make the error, "false" if not, and "cannot say" if they were not certain. The principal sat behind the group so that she could see and count the hands that went up, and the facilitator wrote the numbers on a chart. No comments were made during the voting. The results were as follows:

Errors Made by Ruth Anderson
(Judges = 40)

	True	*False*	*Cannot Say*
1. Too bossy; arbitrary	35	2	3
2. Too loud; forceful	34	3	3
3. Does not listen	27	8	5
4. Interrupts too much	25	8	7
5. Not willing to compromise	25	9	6
6. Too aggressive	25	3	13
7. Not friendly	21	10	7
8. Too abrupt	20	15	5
9. Talks too much	18	5	13
10. Insulting	16	3	21
11. Uses bad language	15	0	25
12. Not cooperative	11	13	16
13. Not sympathetic	9	19	12
14. Does not understand other person	6	23	11
15. Does not understand situation	5	25	10
16. Not interested in people	4	10	26
17. Hostile attitude	3	10	27
18. Cruel	2	30	8

The first eight of these eighteen statements, which received at least one-half the votes, were duplicated to form an analysis check list for the principal. When she role played other situations, the observers checked any items that appeared. To prevent the principal from deliberately controlling herself during the sessions, they were rather lengthy (about twenty minutes), the situations were imperfectly described so that she would not know what to expect, new antagonists were brought into the scene unexpectedly, and the antagonists (teachers) were instructed to deliberately behave so as to upset the principal and cause her to operate in a manner for which she had been criticized previously.

After every session, the check marks were totaled and charted; in this way the principal's progress was monitored.

Impersonal Purposes

Up to this point emphasis has been placed on role playing in terms of individuals. Role playing also can be done to evaluate *procedures*, regardless of individuals. For example, a sales presentation can be analyzed and evaluated through role playing.

Assessment Centers

One of the more recent applications of role playing in evaluation and testing is within the framework of an assessment center. The assessment center combines paper-and-pencil tests and new action testing and evaluation methods. The assessment is an ongoing process involving simulations, interaction exercises, and a variety of small-group tasks over a period of at least two days and often as long as five or six days. The most recent and increasingly popular application of the methodology is in the selection and development of managers. Often first- and second-level supervisors attend assessment centers as part of their developmental and training experience. The center fulfills two objectives: first, it provides data from which the organization (upper-level management) can make informed decisions regarding the promotability and developmental needs of participants; second, it assists the participant in identifying areas in which improvement is possible and in assessing his or her own personal and managerial resources.

Assessment centers can be traced to two basic sources. The first source is psychometrics or psychological testing. In part, an assessment center is an extension of the testing process in which specific factors related to performance are identified and standardized. As is the case in any effective testing situation, the instruments and processes utilized must be validated and checked for reliability; i.e., it must be clear that the instrument measures the factors it is designed to measure and measures them consistently over time.

The second source is situation testing. Situation testing can be traced back to applications in para-military situations (OSS, 1948) and from the early work of

J. L. Moreno (1953). In the early development of situation testing, individuals were given tasks and/or roles to carry out, and their performance was observed and analyzed. Based on their ability to carry out a given role or execute a given task, judgments were made about their capacities. In early situation testing there was little opportunity to validate the accuracy of the experiential process in predicting actual performance on the job or in a social context. For example, at his institute in Beacon, New York, the late J. L. Moreno demonstrated situation-testing techniques for assessing the readiness of mental patients to return to society. The patient would role play a job interview or a discussion with a parent or sibling in the training environment, with group members playing the roles of various individuals who were part of the patient's back-home milieu. Although there was no clear-cut validation of this process, the facilitator and group members often could observe that the patient was not ready to handle a typical family or job situation, that additional treatment and training experiences were necessary.

These two methodologies—psychometric testing and situation testing— have been combined in assessment center procedures. Large organizations are expending a great deal of effort in developing a variety of interactive and social testing experiences that can be used to predict performance on the job and in higher levels of authority. The appropriateness of role playing as a testing or evaluating device depends in large measure on a sound theoretical basis for formulating the testing procedure.

SUMMARY

In life we learn to play our roles, and we "freeze" into patterns that become so habitual we are not really aware of what we do. We can see others more clearly than we can see ourselves and vice-versa. To learn what we do is the first step for improvement. To accept the validity of the judgments of others is the second step. To want to change is the third step. To practice new behaviors under guided supervision and with constant feedback is the fourth step. To use these new patterns in daily life is the last step. Role playing used for analysis follows these general steps and leads to training.

Role playing is particularly appropriate for evaluation because spontaneous behavior is more "veridical"—or true—than other testing behavior for some types of evaluation and so can give quick and accurate estimates of complex functioning.

REFERENCES

Borgatta, E. F. Analysis of social interaction: Actual, role playing and projective. *Journal of Abnormal and Social Psychology*, 1956, 40, 190-196.

Moreno, J. L. *Who shall survive?* Beacon, NY: Beacon House, 1953.

Office of Strategic Services, Assessment Staff. *Assessment of men.* New York: Holt, Rinehart and Winston, 1948.

10

Modifying Behavior

THE STIMULUS-RESPONSE APPROACH TO BEHAVIOR CHANGE

Behavior modification is based on "stimulus-response" theory. The behavior modification strategy is simple: by introducing appropriate stimuli one can produce predictable responses. By experimenting with various stimuli and manipulating the stimuli to produce desired results, one can produce new behaviors and new patterns of action. These patterns, in turn, can be reinforced and supported by various rewards, and undesired behavior can be eliminated by applying negative consequences.

The history of behavior modification is complex and touches a wide range of issues. B. F. Skinner (1938) applied operant conditioning (stimulus-response theory) in a technique that became known as programed instruction and that was used systematically to introduce information in a carefully structured set of procedures. Psychologists of the school known as "behaviorists" began applying stimulus-response theory to a wide range of emotional and social problems. As stimulus-response methodology became more sophisticated and as behavior modification theories were applied to interpersonal affairs, it became clear that the key issue in most managerial and interpersonal situations was the individual's capacity to interact effectively with others. Although programed instruction could move people from one level of knowledge to another, it could not provide them with the understanding and insight that comes from actually trying out new behavior in ongoing human situations. Similarly, although programmatic approaches to human affairs might increase the individual's knowledge and skill in dealing with management and interpersonal problems, it became clear that the best way to learn and reinforce interpersonal skills was to try them out, to practice them. Such practice requires that two or more people interact with each other in order to test, validate, and reinforce the learning process.

Role playing has become an integral part of the behaviorist's approach to learning. Role playing provides opportunities for introducing new stimuli and evoking new responses; it provides opportunities for reinforcing desired behavior and diminishing or eliminating undesired behavior; it provides opportunities for learning by doing. Role playing and behavior modification share many theoretical bases.

1. Behavioral change occurs as a result of behaving. Talking about behavior, analyzing behavior, exploring attitudes, and providing new information are not optimum learning strategies. The best way to develop new behavior is to try it out and then obtain reinforcement and support for useful and appropriate action.

2. The major concern in behavior modification strategies is the "here-and-now." The key questions are "How can I respond appropriately to the situation with which I am confronted?" and "How can I act in ways that provide fulfillment and rewards?" Role playing, too, is concerned with action, with the here-and-now. Neither approach is designed to analyze the past or intellectualize about the present. Both methodologies are concerned primarily with behavior, not emotions or thoughts.

3. In most forms of behavior modification there is immediate feedback. For example, in programed instruction the student is immediately made aware if he or she has not provided the right answer for a given question. With this immediate feedback, the student can check his or her work and correct mistakes on the spot. In therapeutic techniques in which desired behavior is evoked, reinforcement occurs in close proximity. Thus, a teacher or therapist hugs a child immediately after the child has behaved in an appropriate way; the hug occurs as soon as the desired behavior occurs. Similarly, in role playing, if an individual acts appropriately in response to another, he or she immediately receives the positive consequences of that act.

4. Behavior modification relies heavily on reinforcement in order to sustain and support new behavior. Thus, in trying to change the behavior patterns of young and disturbed children, specific routines are repeated over and over again and reinforced by a variety of rewards. Similarly, in role playing it is useful and desirable to have participants try out new behavior more than once to reinforce that new behavior through role rotation, role reversal, post-session analysis, and other methods that increase repetition and reinforcement.

Given these similarities in strategy and method it is inevitable that role playing and behavior modification should move closer together. The specific applications of behavior modification when integrated with role playing are *behavior rehearsal* and *behavior modeling*. Both of these techniques are essentially role-play techniques that draw heavily on behavior modification (stimulus-response) theory and techniques.

BEHAVIOR REHEARSAL

In behavior rehearsal an individual is asked to deal with a specific problem that has been identified through small-group discussion, a problem census, a presentation, or the individual's own analysis of areas in which he or she wishes to practice and improve. In most instances some ground rules or procedures are introduced to aid the individual in coping with the situation under consideration. For example, the facilitator may present a framework for dealing with resistance or hostility, including ground rules such as:

1. When resistance or hostility occurs, it is important to understand the nature of the resistance. Therefore, listen to the other person, try to elicit his or her ideas or feelings, and do not criticize or make fun of the other person.
2. Try not to do anything to increase the resistance or conflict.
3. Express your own point of view clearly and without hostility.

This specific set of guidelines may not be appropriate for every situation. The key issue, however, is that in dealing with a wide range of managerial, interpersonal, and social issues it is important for practitioners and students to establish some criteria for determining whether a particular behavior or set of behaviors is appropriate and effective. For example, sales representatives may practice responding to a predictable objection, and a criterion for effectiveness may be that their responses encourage the buyer to make a positive decision by reducing doubts about the product. Teachers may agree that when dealing with a resistant or unruly student the desired response is one that does not alienate or "put down" the student and at the same time does not diminish the integrity of the teacher. Nurses may agree that the critical criteria for dealing with a hostile patient include the ability to respond to the patient in a way that reduces his or her tension and hostility while maintaining a proper level of treatment or patient care.

The Procedural Framework

There are almost endless areas in interpersonal and managerial affairs in which practice and rehearsal are desirable. Thus, the facilitator's function in many instances is to aid the individual's identification of key problems (or to introduce problems that have been identified through training-needs analyses, interviews, or other methods) and to provide a framework within which the participant can practice and improve his or her skills in responding to the specific situation. Whether the issue is handling union grievances or soliciting key community members for funds or involvement in political activity, the methodology is consistent.

Identify key issues or problems within the framework of the topic or agenda for the session. For example, the issue might be in an educational setting: dealing with overactive or unruly students in an elementary school classroom.

Develop guidelines or a framework for assessing and feeding back the impact of the participants' behavior. For example, "Do not alienate the student, but also remain consistent and maintain your own integrity and self-esteem."

Have participants identify a specific situation with which they have dealt unsuccessfully or an anticipated situation for which they want to prepare. For example, the facilitator may suggest that each individual think of a classroom situation in which he or she had difficulty with a resistant individual and in which that difficulty was not satisfactorily resolved.

Split the group into small "rehearsal" groups. There may be as few as three or as many as seven or eight people in each rehearsal team.

Provide a specific, clear-cut, and repeatable rehearsal procedure so that all participants have the opportunity to practice dealing with the problem situation they have identified. For example, in a team of three participants, member A plays her own role and member B plays the student. Member C is the observer. Participant A makes an affirmative statement to the student and gets feedback regarding her behavior in that situation. She has a chance to try the situation again and to get additional feedback. In most instances, a third or fourth try is built into the process. Where appropriate, one or two group members can be briefed by the key participant on the kind of resistance or hostility that may be encountered; thus the target participant can first practice her response without resistance or interruption. As she builds confidence and obtains feedback and reinforcement, a third or fourth try can be made in which resistance is introduced in the form of a second role player who argues back or hassles member A, thus providing an opportunity for member A to test her responses in increasingly realistic interactions.

Provide a format for feedback. In addition to rehearsing or trying out behavior and experiencing conflict, participants also must obtain feedback. It is usually desirable to establish a firm and clear-cut format for giving and receiving feedback. For example, in the case of the "unruly student" problem, the following ground rules might apply:

1. After an individual has tried out a piece of behavior for dealing with the unruly student, she receives positive feedback from all members of the rehearsal team.
2. After positive feedback has been given, the individual has an opportunity to "self-correct" or make observations about her satisfaction or dissatisfaction with the behavior she has tried out.

3. Finally, a second round of feedback occurs within the group, and rehearsal-team members give improvement feedback: suggestions, recommendations, alternatives, and so on. Some of this feedback may be critical, but it is aimed at increasing the individual's capacity to deal with the situation and in a setting in which she has an opportunity to try again and take advantage of the feedback. Thus, someone in the group might say, "It seemed to me that in dealing with this student you had an edge in your voice and generally seemed ready to get tough. My suggestion is that you might be a little more open or relaxed without knuckling under." The target participant may choose to utilize this feedback, modify it, or in one way or another experiment with it, but need not accept it as given. The frame of reference of the entire process is that participants within the group are resources for the target player. She can use those resources to develop alternative courses of action, experiment with new behavior, or reinforce and confirm existing patterns of behavior.

In some situations the behavior rehearsal can be handled much more informally. For example, a supervisor might say to his boss, "I am a little concerned about dealing with the Federal inspector who is going to visit the plant today. I know he is going to ask some questions about product quality and I am going to have difficulty answering them." The boss might then say, "Well, let's try it out." To do this, the boss might play the role of the inspector and ask tough questions, giving the supervisor a chance to try out answers. Feedback might then be given and the supervisor might have a second try at handling the situation. The learning situation might be made slightly more formal by bringing in additional people and trying to predict possible resistances or arguments that the Federal inspector might pose. The supervisor can then practice any point about which he feels unsure or unclear.

The wedding of role playing and behavior modification in behavior rehearsal is successful because it combines highly desirable learning opportunities. Specifically, participants have a chance to learn how to behave more effectively by actually behaving rather than talking about behavior. They receive reinforcement when their behavior appears effective to their colleagues, and they may receive "negative" feedback when their behavior seems inappropriate. There is ample opportunity for repetition; however, unlike the more traditional and programmatic forms of behavior modification, there is also the opportunity for a great deal of experimentation and spontaneity.

BEHAVIOR MODELING

Behavior modeling is another form of behavior modification. It contains many of the elements present in behavior rehearsal. There is opportunity for reinforcement, repetition, and immediate feedback. The roots of behavior modeling are in therapy. In working with patients in clinical or therapeutic settings, psychologists found that a patient's inability to handle a given situation was in part due to the fact that he or she did not know how the situation could or should be handled. In effect, the patient had no model, no framework for action in dealing with the situation. In some instances, these difficulties were the result of clear-cut disabilities in which the individual simply had not had an opportunity to experience a particular piece of behavior because of physical or psychological limitations. For example, an individual with a speech problem might need the opportunity to observe someone forming words slowly and definitively in order to practice a skill that he or she had never been able to develop. Everyone has experienced behavior modeling in day-to-day situations, without the label and perhaps without a formal, structured approach; e.g., children learn to talk in part by modeling the behavior of their parents.

As behavior modeling became increasingly popular in nontherapeutic situations, as it moved into industry, government, and public agencies, new formats and techniques were introduced. Whereas behavior modeling in its earliest forms was done simply by having a teacher, therapist, or trainer demonstrate desired behavior, as more complex and organizationally based problems were faced, it became clear that various frameworks and ground rules needed to be introduced. The issue was not simply "do it as I do it," but rather, in many institutional settings, the issue became "do it in a way that is consistent with company policy and sound practice and that ensures equal treatment and responsiveness to others."

There are many opportunities for variation in the way in which a grievance or complaint from a customer, an employee, or a union is handled. However, in each case there are policies and desirable human relations techniques to be considered. Thus, it is desirable to provide a procedural or step-by-step process that is in itself a model of what can or should be done. The model will vary depending on the organizational environment. In an example—generalized to provide broad opportunities for application—the model is first presented as a step-by-step outline in written form. Participants then see the model portrayed on videotape or film. This is referred to as a *behavioral display*. It is important that the portrayal is worked through carefully to ensure that it is consistent with sound policy and effective practices in the area under consideration.

Secondly, it is desirable to have the behavioral display portrayed by authentic, experienced managers rather than by actors who do not bring their own experiences to the situation. Most facilitators find that the development of effective television or film displays requires a great deal of training and practice on the part of those acting out the interaction to ensure that it is handled effectively.

The following is a step-by-step procedural model for handling complaints as it would be presented to a training group.

1. Clarify the complaint. Seek information without hostility, argument, or evaluation.
2. Be sure that you understand the complaint. Restate it. Show that you understand it.

3. State your position (the organizational policy) on the issue.

4. Recommend a course of action.

The presentation of the procedural model would be followed by an audiovisual behavioral display.

Administrator: I understand that you wanted to talk to me about the change in your assignment.

Employee (or volunteer): Yes, I had made plans based on the schedule suggested earlier in the year, and the new schedule makes it impossible for me to do some things that I have counted on.

Administrator: Tell me a little more about how the schedule affects you.

Employee: Well, I had made special arrangements to pick up one of my children after school, and that fit in with my old work schedule and assignments.

Administrator: I understand—the schedule and assignments just developed mean that your previous plans aren't working out. Is that your basic problem with the new arrangement?

Employee: Yes. If I could work out something that would permit me to pick up my children, I wouldn't have a problem with the schedule.

Administrator: In order to ensure consistent and fair allocation of activities, work assignments of this type are based on seniority. Persons with more service have the option to choose certain assignments and schedules.

Employee: Yes, that is clear, but it seems to me that my situation merits some special consideration. I have always done my work well and have been on time, and this is a very important family problem, not simply a whim.

Administrator: I understand, and I do want to be clear that the policy was set after experimentation with other ways of handling scheduling and assignments. As you know, there are a lot of people involved and each person needs to know that there is a clear and predictable range of policies that can be relied on.

Employee: Yes, that's clear. It just seems that something could be done.

Administrator: I can suggest a couple of alternatives. One is that it is possible for another member of the group to switch assignments with you. That would have to be on a voluntary basis. However, if you are unable to get someone to switch schedules with you, you may want to consider some temporary arrangement with a babysitter or day-care center. That is, of course, your personal decision. However, the policy is clear and necessary in order to meet the needs and expectations of the largest number of employees possible. I suggest that we talk again in a couple of days after you have had a chance to explore some of the alternatives that might be available.

After a procedural model and behavioral display have been presented, group members try out their own effectiveness in dealing with the issue. Two basic approaches can be applied in utilizing role playing for trying out a procedural or behavioral model and for increasing personal skill and effectiveness: (a) structured role playing and (b) unstructured or spontaneous role playing.

Structured Role Playing

A carefully constructed role play can be used to provide an opportunity for people to practice and experiment with a specific set of skills or procedures. Typically, an observer guide or feedback format is also utilized so that participants have a chance to try out a new procedure or behavior, receive feedback, and practice the procedure again. The second practice can be achieved by repeating the original role play or by trying a new role play. A final option is for the individual to move from a structured role play into a developmental role play dealing with the situation that he or she is actually experiencing. The following is an example of a structured role play dealing with the issue of resistance.

DEALING WITH COMPLAINTS

Instructions (for the facilitator)

1. The activity is to be conducted by teams of three. If necessary, teams of four can be used with two people acting as observers.
2. Distribute role descriptions and an observer guide to each group member. Tell the members that they will practice the specific steps and skills involved in dealing with a complaint or with resistance from a subordinate, associate, or customer.
3. Post the four-step model below so that it can be seen by all. Announce that the model is to be followed by the person handling the complaint.

The Model

1. Clarify the complaint. Seek information without hostility, argument, or evaluation.
2. Be sure that you understand the complaint. Restate it. Show that you understand it.
3. State your position (the organizational policy) on the issue.
4. Recommend a course of action.

Role for Lee Phillips, Coordinator of Voluntary Programs

You are Lee Phillips, a paid staff member of an organization made up primarily of volunteer members. The organization provides a variety of social and charitable services; part of its activity is raising funds for these services. Voluntary members or associates engage in fund raising. Volunteer team and community captains are asked to coordinate the efforts of other fund raisers on a neighborhood basis. Your concern is that you have no direct authority or power over the volunteers, and they are often unresponsive to guidance and direction that does not fit in with their personal plans. Also they often have complaints or concerns about goals, quotas, and procedures, and part of your job is to respond to these complaints and to provide effective guidance and direction.

You are about to be approached by a team captain who has several objections to the fund-raising arrangements this year. The captain evidently does not like the idea of volunteers making direct requests for more money. All your professional experience has shown that fund raising is more effective when people have the courage and conviction to request a specific amount of money and to indicate the need for an increased donation. If left to their own devices, most people tend to give the same amount as last year, or less. Therefore, it is important for fund raisers to find ways to ask for an increase, and, again, experience shows that the more specific they are, the better chance they have of getting the desired results. The direct approach is a matter of organizational policy. You are an administrator in this organization as well as a staff person and you have the responsibility to implement established policies.

This year the organization's goal is to increase donations by 10 percent.

Role for Dale McKenzie, Fund-Raising Volunteer

You are Dale McKenzie. You have devoted part of your time each year to helping a charitable organization raise funds. You have agreed to serve as a team captain and have six people working with you in making direct solicitations to local residents and business people. It has been recommended that during this current fund-raising campaign specific goals or targets be set for each team and that these, in part, should be based on an increase of 10 percent over past donations and on an increase in the number of new donors. Under the proposed procedure, each fund raiser is asked to specify a given amount when he or she is soliciting a resident or local business person. For example, if Sam Jones gave $100 last year, the fund raiser is to open the conversation by indicating that $110 would be appropriate this year, based on the increasing needs of the organization.

Quite a few of the people on your team have complained that they do not like to ask for a specific amount of money. They are dealing with friends and neighbors, and they do not want to impose on them. They feel that each person should give in accordance with his or her own feelings and beliefs and that their job is not to put pressure on people but merely to provide an opportunity for them to give.

You have received a lot of bulletins and instructions indicating that fund raisers should specify a dollar amount and that it should be 10 percent more than what was donated last year. You don't like this idea and are resistant to it. On the other hand, you don't want to go ahead and change the ground rules without discussing it with the staff person from the organization who is responsible for your team. You want to meet with that staff person and resolve this issue for both yourself and the members of your team.

Observer Guide

Below you will find an outline of the step-by-step model that was presented earlier. You will now be observing two people—one an administrator in a charitable organization and the other a volunteer team captain—discussing a complaint that the team captain has about the organization's policy. You are to pay particular attention to the procedural model that was described earlier and to give feedback to the administrator regarding his or her method of handling the complaint. The model is shown below.

In Column 2 identify what was said regarding each of the key steps in the model; i.e., did the administrator seek clarification and, if so, how? Did he or she show understanding? If so, how? In Column 3 indicate the suggestions or alternative courses of action that you feel would be desirable.

Procedure	What Was Said	Suggestions and Alternatives
1. *Clarify the complaint* (Seek information, avoid hostility)		
2. *Show that you understand* (Restate the complaint)		
3. *State your position* (Policy)		
4. *Recommend a course of action*		

Unstructured or Spontaneous Role Playing

The second procedure permits participants to handle a real-life problem, applying the behavioral model or procedure to issues with which they are involved or expect to be involved in the near future. Once again, the procedural model is presented and the audiovisual display shown. The next step may be to have participants enact a structured role play. They may then move to a situation of their own choosing so they can try out the model and new behavior in reference to a real, back-home situation. In this way, group members can change roles and obtain experience in handling prepared cases as well as in dealing with more spontaneous situations.

In unstructured role playing, one participant in each subgroup is designated to try out the model using a problem of his or her choice. The participant is instructed to give a very brief description of the situation and a very brief indication of the nature of the resistance or complaint that will be encountered. A second group member is chosen to play the role of the individual bringing the complaint to the first participant. He or she is encouraged to utilize as much information as has been made available and, if necessary, to improvise, providing the kind of resistance that appears most realistic based on his or her own experience. For example, in a group of professional fund raisers, all members of the group are familiar with the complaints and resistances that are encountered in the field. The persons involved enact the complaint-handling process, and an observer is assigned to use as an observer guide. Complex and sophisticated guides can be developed to meet the needs of the group and the issues being confronted.

FOLLOW-UP SESSIONS AND PROCEDURES

Very often, as group members become involved in working through a behavioral model or procedure, they begin to identify critical issues that they face in their work or social situations. When small groups are involved, the facilitator can move from the prepared role plays and multiple role-play techniques into more spontaneous enactments. Depending on the skill and experience of the facilitator, various behavior rehearsal and behavior modeling techniques can be applied to aid individuals in coping with difficult issues. For example, the facilitator may model given behaviors as they apply to problem situations faced by group members. Alternatively, group members who have had positive experiences in handling critical issues may be asked to model behavior for other group members as a basis for additional experimentation and skill practice.

The facilitator may move from a behavior modeling activity to behavior rehearsal, thus providing participants with an opportunity to continue trying out key steps of a given procedure and receiving feedback on those key steps. For example, some group members may have a great deal of difficulty showing understanding when they disagree with another person's position. A behavior rehearsal approach can be used to give these participants a chance to show understanding when encountering resistance, to receive feedback on their effectiveness, to try again, and to deal with resistance while continuing the behavior rehearsal cycle.

SUMMARY

In combining behavior modification with role-play techniques, new training methods have emerged. Two of the most popular and useful methods are behavior rehearsals and behavior modeling. Both of these methods provide opportunities for participants to examine their own behavior and to modify their behavior based on new stimuli. In large measure, these stimuli are provided by various forms of interaction; that is, participants try out new behavior in accordance with suggested guidelines, frameworks, and procedural or behavioral models. They often are asked to repeat a step or procedure until they become more facile in its application. They receive feedback that reinforces positive behavior and usually diminishes negative or ineffective behavior. The use of written procedural models, audiovisual techniques, and observer guides provides additional reinforcement and opportunities for experimentation.

Combining behavior modification techniques with role-playing techniques makes it possible to organize and systematize some aspects of the learning situation while at the same time providing opportunities for experimentation and spontaneous interaction.

REFERENCE

Skinner, B. F. *The behavior of organisms: An experimental analysis.* New York: Appleton-Century-Crofts, 1938.

ANNOTATED BIBLIOGRAPHY

Annotated Bibliography

Anonymous. Industrial psychology pays in this plant. *Dun's Review & Modern Industry*, 1948, *16*, 67-68.

Dr. Alfred J. Marrow, a psychologist and president of the Harwood Corporation, uses psychological techniques in running his company. Examples are given of how role playing is used to improve communications and problem solving.

Anonymous. Act it, learn it. *Business Week*, April 9, 1949, 96-103.

Foremen use role playing to improve social skills. The American Type Founders Company is one of the first organizations to use industrial role playing. The general phases are: (a) foremen meet to determine principles of behavior, (b) a foreman in training is briefed on a sample problem, (c) two workers meet this foreman and act out the problem, (d) the session is recorded, and (e) a post-role-play discussion is conducted.

Anonymous. Acting that teaches how to handle people. *Dun's Review & Modern Industry*, 1949, *17*, 50-52.

Role playing has long been used as a demonstration and training method in sales development. Its value is based on the dictum that we learn best by actually doing. In role playing for training, the situation should be realistic and slightly difficult to solve. Role playing is a superior procedure for conveying messages and is much superior to written language in avoiding equivocality. Role playing helps people to understand how others think and feel, which is the beginning of good morale in industrial leadership.

Anonymous. Role playing pays off for Ethyl. *Sales Management*, 1953, 71, 41.

Salesmen at the Ethyl Corporation were trained by playing roles which were recorded and then played back.

Anonymous. Role playing in training supervisors. *Factory Management and Maintenance*, 1954, *112*, 102-105.

A summary and analysis of 107 replies to a questionnaire about industrial role playing that was originally sent to 445 training directors.

Anonymous. 64 hints to help you make role playing work. *Factory Management and Maintenance*, 1954, *112*, 282-290.

> Sixty-four hints from comments made on a questionnaire returned by 107 training directors who use role playing. Samples: (1) Give participants a full understanding of what they are going to do; (64) Help players to save face.

Anonymous. Role playing. *Industrial Distribution*, September 1957, 113-136.

> Role playing in sales training accomplishes these purposes: reality testing by using true-to-life situations; learning by doing; seeing another's point of view; handling problems on the spot; solving problems through people; obtaining full participation; and affecting attitudes. Role playing is used (a) to teach fundamentals, (b) for specific sales problems, (c) for sales problems within the company, (d) to train phone and counter salesmen, (e) to train sales supervisors, (f) for general skill practice, and (g) to practice human relations skills. Pitfalls and booby traps in directing role playing are discussed.

Argyris, C. *Role playing in action.* Bulletin No. 16, New York State School of Industrial and Labor Relations, Cornell University, May, 1951.

> Argyris covers the general purposes of role playing, including a definition and where role playing can be used; discusses its value and why it is valuable in re-education; tells how to prepare for role playing, including identifying problems and getting the members to want to experience a change; and tells how to help the group to observe and evaluate role playing. The last section contains suggestions for the practical use of role playing as a training technique, covers areas of resistance, and gives a number of hints about role-playing procedures.

Barron, M. E. Role practice in interview training. *Sociatry*, 1947, *1*, 198-208.

> Role playing can be used for the effective transference of principles into methods. Because the interview is a kind of unrehearsed play between two persons, role-playing methods are particularly appropriate in training interviewers. After a practice session, trainees evaluate an interview and then practice themselves.

Bavelas, A. Role playing and management training. *Sociatry*, 1947, *1*, 183-191.

> This is a pioneer article about role playing in industry. Bavelas suggests a procedure with fourteen steps:
>
> 1. A short discussion of problem area is conducted.
> 2. Two protagonists (leaders) are removed from group (X and Y).
> 3. The problem to be played is described by the leader.
> 4. A "worker" is selected from remaining group members.
> 5. The "worker" is prepared for his role.
> 6. Props are set.
> 7. One protagonist is called in and given instructions.
> 8. The leader stops the session when indicated.
> 9. X returns to the group and becomes an observer.
> 10. Y is now called in and interacts with "worker."
> 11. The leader summarizes.
> 12. X and Y are asked for their reactions; the "worker" also responds.
> 13. The group holds a general discussion.
> 14. A new member (Z) is asked to replay the leader role.

Beckhard, R. Role playing: Do it yourself technique. *Sales Management*, 1956, 76, 27-29.

Instructions are given for using role playing in the training of salesmen. General dos and don'ts are offered.

Blake, R. R. Experimental psychodrama with children. *Group Psychotherapy*, 1955, 8, 347-350.

Blake discusses how children can best learn new social skills through the use of role playing.

Blansfield, M. G. Consider "value analysis" to get the most out of role playing. *Personnel Journal*, 1953, 34, 251-254.

Role playing can be relatively ineffective unless "value analysis" is used. Some system of identifying and rating important variables of role playing should be used. On the basis of experience with training groups, the author found fifteen areas useful for evaluation.

Blansfield, M. G. Role playing as a method in executive development. *Journal of Personnel Administration and Industrial Relations*, 1954, 1, 131-135.

Role playing has three major purposes: changing behavior, giving information, and learning techniques for problem solving.

Blansfield, M. G. Role playing: A suggested method of introduction to training groups. *Journal of the American Society of Training Directors*, 1957, 11(1), 19-22.

Resistance to role playing usually is based on insecurity or the fear of ridicule. However, the stress and tension of participation is an aid to learning if handled properly. The writer suggests these rules:
1. Do not formalize and frighten the participants.
2. Avoid terms such as "role playing" and "psychodrama."
3. Get the group relaxed, and do not force role playing.
4. Avoid too many preliminaries.
5. Use multiple role playing first, getting the whole group to work in pairs.
6. Use a written problem.
7. Use team observers.
8. Use buzz groups for discussions.

Boguslaw, R., & Bach, G. R. "Work culture management" in industry: A role for the social science consultant. *Group Psychotherapy*, 1959, 12, 134-142.

The special conditions of a formally organized work environment and the objectives and operations of social-science consultants working within the industrial framework are discussed. Through the use of role-playing techniques, work-group members are given an opportunity to understand and discuss the inadequacies of their previous behavior. Role playing is more effective when the group members are familiar with the definitions of the appropriate goals, roles, and activities for the group.

Bohart, A. C. Role playing and interpersonal conflict reduction. *Journal of Counseling Psychology*, 1977, 24, 15-24.

With a group of eighty undergraduate females, using four procedures, role playing was found most effective for reducing anger and changing hostile attitudes.

Borgatta, E. F. Analysis of social interaction: Actual, role playing and projective. *Journal of Abnormal and Social Psychology*, 1956, *40*, 190-196.

A group of subjects were evaluated in terms of actual behavior, role-playing behavior, and pencil-and-paper tests. It appeared that predictions from tests to actual or role-playing behavior were weak, and that considerable caution should be exercised in attempting to predict from verbal to action behavior. On the other hand, role playing appeared to give the same kind of information obtained from observations of unrehearsed actual behavior.

Bradford, L. P. Supervisory training as a diagnostic instrument. *Personnel Administration*, 1945, *8*, 3-7.

Supervisory training necessarily contains diagnosis. Using role playing as an auxiliary method, the author found that because acting is spontaneous, attitudes are revealed. Techniques of handling problems are well illustrated in this manner. Participants tend to choose problems that are meaningful for them.

Bradford, L. P., & Lippitt, R. Role playing in supervisory training. *Personnel*, 1946, *27*, 358-369.

While training in industry has been remarkably successful in affecting work skills, it has been unsuccessful in changing the human relations ability of supervisors. ". . . exhortations will never transmit the finger dexterity essential to operate a typewriter but we evidently feel a foreman can be taught to handle situations . . ." An outline of a typical training session is given. The role-playing director's skill depends on his ability to select appropriate scenes, set the scenes to develop what is important, know when to cut off the action, and lead post-role-play discussions.

Branzel, R. Role playing as a training device in preparing multiple-handicapped youth for employment. *Group Psychotherapy*, 1963, *16*, 16-21.

Role playing is one of the most efficient ways to prepare handicapped youths to locate and hold jobs. Better means of interviewing, better behavior patterns, and better general attitudes toward self and others are developed through this action technique.

Broaded, C. H. A statement of the practical application of role playing as a training device. *Sociometry*, 1951, *14*, 69-70.

Role playing supplemented by "how to" material is superior to a procedure that concerns itself only with human relations interactions.

Bronfenbrenner, U., & Newcomb, T. M. Improvisations—An application of psychodrama in personality diagnosis. *Sociatry*, 1948, *1*, 367-382.

A discussion of the use of role playing for testing by the Office of Strategic Services during World War II. In addition to judging participants, judges themselves were judged for capacity to evaluate others. The "cases" or "plots" were modified in many cases to suit the individuals involved. Similar procedures were used in a study to predict successful clinical psychologists for the Veterans Administration. In the test, verbal content, character of voice, and bodily movements were considered important variables. A standard set of six common human-conflict situations also is outlined.

Burns, R. K., & Corsini, R. J. The IDEAS technique. *Group Psychotherapy*, 1959, *12*, 175-178.

The IDEAS technique has five parts: I—the Introduction, in which the conference leader lectures on the problem; D—a role-playing Demonstration by trained assistants or members of the group; E—an Enactment by members through multiple role playing; A-Action, or the demonstration to the group by subgroups of what they have done; and S—Summary, the leader's final integration of the session.

Calhoon, R. P. Role playing as a technique for business. *Michigan Business Review*, 1950, *2*(6), 29-32.

Role playing has been used for sales training for many years. Among its values are revealing how lines of reasoning sound in practice, anticipating problems, and helping to make timing more effective. Role playing attacks the problem of attitudes more directly than any other method. Among its advantages are that it uses down-to-earth situations, helps to develop practical solutions, and brings out weaknesses in any human relations problem.

Clore, G. L., & Jeffery, K. M. *Emotional role playing, attitude change and attraction toward a disabled person.* Paper presented at the Midwestern Psychological Association Convention, Detroit, MI, May 6-8, 1971.

Emotional attitudes toward the disabled were changed in a positive direction when students were asked to sit in a wheelchair for an hour.

Cohen, J. The technique of role-reversal: A preliminary note. *Occupational Psychology*, 1951, *25*, 64-66.

Role reversal is a technique that helps A decide whether B really understands him and helps B learn whether he can restate A's propositions to A's satisfaction. The author claims that "the effort to understand is the beginning of reconciliation" and recommends role reversal for such purposes.

Corsini, R. J. The roleplaying technique in business and industry. (Occasional Paper No. 9.) Chicago: Industrial Relations Center, April 1957.

Role playing has three major uses: diagnostic, training, and instructional. A variety of procedures are available; they call for a sensitive, well-trained leader. Some procedures and typical cases are illustrated.

Corsini, R. J. Roleplaying: Its use in industry. *Advanced Management*, 1960, *25*(2), 20-23.

Role playing has three primary functions: to train (by experiencing), to instruct (via observation), and to evaluate (through critical observation). Its essential value lies in the simultaneous use of the three primary modalities of action, thought, and emotion, which makes a role-playing situation holistic, spontaneous, and natural. A case example of the use of role playing in training an executive is cited.

Corsini, R. J. *Roleplaying in psychotherapy: A manual.* Chicago, IL: Aldine, 1966.

Therapeutic role playing is the main concern of this book, which covers role-play theory, processes in diagnosis, instruction, and treatment. Two cases examples and an annotated bibliography by Samuel Cardone complete the book.

Corsini, R. J., & Howard, D. D. Training through roleplaying. *Concept*, 1960, 2(1), 43-46.

Role playing permits participants to practice reality, thus helping them to attain higher levels of on-the-job functioning through self-criticism and through comments by others, which increase awareness.

Corsini, R. J., & Putzey, L. J. *Bibliography of group psychotherapy*. Beacon, NY: Beacon House, 1957.

A bibliography of approximately 1700 items about group psychotherapy, including several hundred about psychotherapeutic role playing (psychodrama). A number of articles about group procedures in industry are indexed.

Ettkin, L., & Snyder, L. A model for peer-group counseling based on role-play. *School Counselor*, 1972, 19, 215-218.

This article describes the use of role playing as a means to promote new social learning through identification with other group members. The concept is that by this means projection of thoughts and feelings can be directed into others.

Fantel, E. Psychodrama in the counseling of industrial personnel. *Sociatry*, 1948, 2, 384-398.

Role playing was used in an industrial situation in which there were management-employee tensions. By acting out various situations, better understanding of the personalities of three salesmen were determined, and a clearer understanding of the problems involved was obtained.

Foley, A. W. Extemporaneous role playing: Its several advantages. *Personnel Journal*, 1955, 34, 177-180.

Extemporaneous role playing—described as situations written on cards, given to subjects to read for one minute and then to act out for two-to-three minutes—has some advantages over "rehearsed" role playing, which tends to be superficial and artificial. After the role play, short discussions were held. This method is valuable in warming up a new group.

Franks, T. W. A note on role playing in an industrial setting. *Group Psychotherapy*, 1952, 5(59), 63.

A description is given of the use of role playing in an industrial problem that included poor communication and ineffective managing techniques. Attitudinal changes occurred rapidly, and this led to better relationships.

Franks, T. W. Project-centered group treatment. *Group Psychotherapy*, 1959, 12, 161-165.

A case history is recounted of an industrial morale problem. First, out of a plant population of one thousand employees, a total of 120 natural leaders were located by asking employees "Who do you think I should talk to . . .? These 120 people were formed into twelve groups of ten members each. Each group met weekly. Care was taken to have heterogeneous groupings. At the end of the sessions, in each of the ten groups a decision was made to accept a plan previously rejected by the employees, which had been the original purpose of the meeting. Role playing was used during the sessions to point out how the plan would work.

French, J. R. P. Retraining an autocratic leader. *Journal of Abnormal and Social Psychology*, 1944, 39, 224-237.

> A discussion of the retraining of an ineffective, autocratic leader of a (Boy Scout) scoutmaster training program. Through role playing before a group of other leaders and by means of discussions, this formerly dull and rigid trainer became more flexible. A description of a session is given.

French, J. R. P. Role playing as a method of training foremen. *Sociometry*, 1945, 8, 410-422.

> Stenographic notes of the handling of an actual problem in training foremen are presented in this article. The advantages of role playing for industrial training are that it is flexible and realistic and stimulates participation, involvement, and identification. It helps trainees by providing concrete, realistic situations, enables the trainer to give immediate coaching, permits diagnostic observations, and leads to sensitivity training.

Gordon, M. Role playing in industry. *Group Psychotherapy*, 1959, 12, 187-191. (Reprinted from *The Wall Street Journal*, March 15, 1957.)

> One way to obtain insight into situations is to role play the parts. A case is cited of an advertising supervisor who sold newspapers on a street corner in order to understand consumers' reactions to a particular newspaper. A number of instances of use of this and more conventional kinds of role playing are given in support of the thesis that role playing can be effective in business and industry.

Gordon, R. M. Interesting modifications on role playing. *Journal of the American Society of Training Directors*, 1956, 10(5), 26-29.

> Two basic principles of effective teaching are practice and participation. Role playing, of all techniques, comes closest to satisfying these demands. The author suggests two variations of multiple role playing, called group role playing and group multiple role playing. In the latter version, the following steps are taken:
> 1. Different roles are assigned to members.
> 2. The characters are grouped and discuss their roles.
> 3. They then act out the roles in role groups.
> 4. There is discussion by the characters.
> 5. The leader summarizes but does not comment.

Haas, R. B. *Role playing and guidance.* Berkeley, CA: Department of Visual Instruction, University of California, 1953. (Film)

> This 16-mm, black-and-white film shows how role playing can be used by a young boy to solve problems. The boy plays the roles of a school principal, his mother, and himself, thereby gaining insight into what causes problems in his life.

Haire, M. Industrial social psychology. In G. Lindzey (Ed.), *Handbook of social psychology* (Vol. 2). Reading, MA: Addison-Wesley, 1954.

> On page 1116, Haire states that role playing has offered a promise of theoretical analysis of roles and their meaning in groups as well as a research tool for investigation of group structure and the role of the individual in the group. In practice none of these have been realized. Role playing has been chiefly a very practical device for accomplishing the particular function of training supervisors.

Hardt, E. New York City workshops successful. *The Journal of Industrial Training*, 1952, 6(1), 18-20.

This is a summary report of a workshop of the National Association of Training Directors that was devoted to role playing. A number of speakers discussed the theory, applications, uses, values, and dangers of this action procedure in industrial use.

Hollister, W. G., & Husband, G. W. Two roleplaying methods of using mental health films and plays. *Mental Health*, 1955, 39, 277-285.

One of these methods is the "feeling with" procedure; the second is the "helping group" method. Each procedure has specific values for a variety of human relations problems.

Huffman, H. The play's the thing. *Business Education World*, 1948, 26, 392-395.

The use of skits in business-education training is discussed.

Hundleby, G., & Zingle, H. Communication of empathy. *Canadian Counselor*, 1975, 9, 148-152.

CUE—communicating, understanding, empathy—is a program involving fourteen eighty-minute lessons in which high school students participated. Results indicate that students who received the training communicated empathically significantly better than did controls.

Huyck, E. T. Teaching for behavioral change. *Humanist Educator*, 1975, 14, 12-20.

Two methods of teaching communication skills were compared: one was the lecture and the other included modeling and practice (observational role playing and training role playing). Statistically significant improvement was noted with the use of role playing.

Jackson, T. A. Role playing in supervisor development. *Journal of Industrial Training*, 1951, 5(2), 6-9.

Industrial training procedures have developed from those in which the trainees were passive auditors to those requiring greater participation. Role playing is a fourth-stage development that emphasizes the practice of applications of good human relations principles. While it is potentially the most valuable training procedure, much depends on the skill of the trainer. Role playing deals primarily with the manner in which things are done. It can reveal to people what they are doing, leading to personal insights that precede personal changes.

Johnson, D. W., & Dustin, R. The initiation of cooperation through role reversal. *Journal of Social Psychology*, 1970, 82, 193-203.

This reports a study in which a negotiator—highly skilled in role-reversal techniques—attempted to induce cooperation in an adversary. Agreements were better in individualistic than in competitive situations.

Kaull, J. L. Combining role playing, case study and incident method for human relations training. *Journal of American Training Directors*, 1954, 8, 16-19.

Traditional lecture methods were found not effective in helping supervisors change behavior, so role playing was tried. The author reports that ". . . follow-through sessions proved exceptionally valuable in demonstrating to first-line supervisors the possible consequences of their behavior."

Kellogg, E. E. A role playing case: How to get the most out of it. *Personnel Journal*, 1954, *33*, 179-183.

This article offers practical suggestions for using role playing in training foremen, especially techniques for getting such individuals to accept this procedure as a legitimate and worthwhile method of learning.

Klein, A. F. *Role playing in leadership training and group problem solving.* New York: Association Press, 1956.

A text for employing group procedures involving role playing. Suited for people interested in becoming conference leaders, it is oriented to practical use.

Lawshe, C. H., Brune, R. L., & Bolda, R. A. What supervisors say about role playing. *Journal of the American Society of Training Directors*, 1958, *12*(8), 3-7.

Forty-five management trainees in three role-playing groups were asked in the fifth session to indicate their attitudes about the procedure, to test the idea that foremen are naturally resistant to role playing. Results were uniformly favorable. For example 75 percent said "no" to the question "Does role playing put you on the spot?" To the question "Do you have to be a born actor to do a good job of role playing?", 95 percent said "no." Eighty-nine percent said "yes" to the question "Does role playing make a problem easier to understand?" Ninety-one percent disagreed with the contention that role playing is more of a game than a training technique; and more people stated that they would rather be the foreman (protagonist, 55 percent) than the employee role player (antagonist, 32 percent) than the 9 percent who said they would prefer merely to be onlookers. The writers concude that role playing does not automatically encounter resistance.

Lippitt, R. The psychodrama in leadership training. *Sociometry*, 1943, *6*, 286-292.

Role playing has these advantages in industrial training: it gives the trainer an opportunity to observe the trainee in action and to diagnose his real-life leadership style; it enables the trainer to focus on the leadership problems of the trainee; it makes it possible for a number of trainees to profit at the same time; it creates an atmosphere of objectivity; it makes it possible to practice new leadership styles and perfect their execution; and it shows how it is possible to anticipate and handle new situations.

Liveright, A. A. Role playing in leadership training. *Personnel Journal*, 1951, *29*, 412-416.

Role playing has been used in training union delegates how to handle grievance procedures. It is valuable to demonstrate how a problem can be handled. Six steps are described: (a) choosing a problem, (b) agreeing on details, (c) defining the roles of the players, (d) defining the roles of the spectators, (e) the role playing itself, and (f) post-session discussion.

Liveright, A. A. Skits in leadership training. *Personnel Journal*, 1951, *30*, 64-66.

Skits are structured situations played before a group with the purpose of illustrating a problem and obtaining discussion. They are not used primarily for the purpose of personal development.

Lonergan, W. G Role playing in an industrial conflict. *Group Psychotherapy*, 1957, *10*, 105-110.

Lonergan reports how role playing was used to effect communication in a strike situation. Management was unable to change the attitudes of foremen with reference to moving certain materials because the foremen felt that the striking employees would regard the move as hostile. When managers role played a board meeting to show their position, the observing foremen finally understood the importance of the various points of view and changed their own opinions.

Lonergan, W. G. Management trainees evaluate role playing. *Journal of the American Society of Training Directors*, 1958, *12*(10), 20-25.

This paper reports the reactions of twenty-five management trainees to role playing. Seventy-eight percent of the comments to ten groups of questions were judged to be favorable to role playing.

Machaver, W. V., & Fischer, F. E. The leader's role in role playing. *Journal of Industrial Training*, 1953, *7*, 6-16.

Role playing is of value not only to direct participants but also to onlookers. The leader of a session must make executive decisions with regard to controlling scenes. The leader must be careful not to use role playing to put across a prepared message, but should permit members to be spontaneous. Recorders and playback are advisable in industrial use.

Maier, N. R. F. Dramatized case material as a springboard for role playing. *Group Psychotherapy*, 1953, *6*, 30-42.

Role playing is valuable for sensitizing persons to the feelings of others, and for developing listening and empathy skills. However, there is frequently resistance to this procedure. A new method of dramatized skits to be read by participants is suggested as a procedure for reducing tensions and for leading to more spontaneous dramatizations of problems.

Maier, N. R. F., & Solem, A. R. Audience role playing: A new method in human relations training. *Human Relations*, 1951, *4*, 279-294.

In ARP the audience is asked to react to an attitude questionnaire, then given a lecture designed to change attitudes. Another attitude sampling is made. Then role playing is done on a related issue, and a further check of attitudes is made. Generally, role playing seems to be much more effective in changing attitudes than are lectures.

Maier, N. R. F., Solem, A. R., & Maier, A. A. *The role-play technique: A handbook for management and leadership practice.* San Diego, CA: University Associates, 1975.

This book contains a short introduction to the use of case material in role playing and twenty structured situations of the single and multiple type, referring to individual and group problems.

Maier, N. R. F., & Zerfoss, L. F. MRP: A technique for training large groups of supervisors and its potential use in social research. *Human Relations*, 1952, *5*, 177-186.

MRP (multiple role playing) is a combination of the Phillips 66 "buzz group" procedure and role playing. It is designed to be used with large groups, broken into smaller groups that role play a described situation simultaneously. A typical problem, with the roles of the individual members, is given in an illustration.

Marrow, A. J. Group meetings pay off. *Business Week*, 1950, *20*, 82-91.

This interview with Dr. Marrow, a psychologist and president of Harwood Manufacturing Company, is in reference to his ideas of dealing with employees. He advocates democratic, group-centered methods and uses role playing for illustration and training.

Massell, M. Setting the training stage for better conferences. *American Business*, 1949, *19*, 14-15.

The case-history method of training indicates the *what* but not the *why* nor the *how*. Some minor matters may be of great importance in human relations, and role playing can point them out. Role playing is a good procedure for initiating discussions. The author indicates how role playing can be used for demonstration and how the leader can then make comments and lead a discussion.

Mayer, J., & Plutchik, R. Group coaching as an adjunct to role playing in human relations training. *Journal of the American Society of Training Directors*, 1957, *11*(5), 44-45.

Three major principles should be used in human relations training: provide participants as much involvement as possible, maintain interest, and relate material to "real-life" situations. The writers describe a procedure, stated to be superior to multiple role playing, that includes the following steps:

1. Written roles are prepared for typical problems.
2. Role players discuss their problems in teams of two. Several sets of role players can be used.
3. The director and the group discuss the situation and what to look for.
4. Teams are called in and interviewed by group resolutions.
5. The group coaches the role players.
6. After demonstrations, there is discussion.

Meyer, A. Spontaneity. *Sociometry*, 1940, *4*, 150-167.

A concentrated discussion of the theoretical aspects of spontaneity as applied to role playing.

Miller, D. C. Introductory demonstrations and applications of three major uses of role playing for business and government administrators. *Sociometry*, 1951, *14*, 45-58, 67-68.

Three uses of industrial role playing that can be demonstrated are: (a) conference techniques for problem solving, (b) techniques for employee selection, and (c) training methods for employers and supervisors. Miller gives fourteen steps for illustrating the first, thirteen for illustrating the second, and twelve steps for illustrating the third method before large groups.

Miller, D. C. A role playing workshop for business and government administrators: Its research implications. *Group Psychotherapy*, 1953, 6, 50-62.

A detailed outline and summary of an intensive one-day workshop in industrial role playing directed at administrator problems is given, along with a discussion of the research implications of role playing.

Moody, K. A. Role playing as a training technique. *Journal of Industrial Training*, 1953, 7, 3-5.

Role playing can serve as a mirror in which participants see themselves. It fosters insight and empathy. It makes intangible concepts concrete. Observing behavior is much more impressive than listening.

Moreno, J. L., & Borgatta, E. F. An experiment with sociodrama and sociometry in industry. *Sociometry*, 1951, 14, 71-104.

This is an outline of a session directed by Dr. Moreno in which industrial problems are elicited and one of them acted out on the psychodrama stage. The session is then analyzed sociometrically.

Nylen, D., Mitchell, J. R., & Stout, A. *Handbook of staff development and human relations training: Materials developed for use in Africa.* Arlington, VA: NTL Institute for Applied Behavioral Science, 1967.

This is a collection of tested materials designed to be used in developing nations, particularly the African nations. Role-play materials are included.

O'Donnell, W. G. Role playing as a practical training technique. *Personnel*, 1952, 9, 275-289.

This is a concentrated summary of the uses, advantages, and limitations of role playing in industrial training. The author gives credit to George Herbert Mead for clarifying the importance of role playing in social psychology. Role playing permits the gap between principles and practice to be seen and then bridged. It is the proconstruction and reconstruction of experience. The article contains a number of practical hints for the most effective uses of role playing in industrial situations.

O'Donnell, W. G. Role playing in training and management development. *Journal of the American Society of Training Directors*, 1954, 8, 76-78.

"It (role playing) is learning by doing under conditions in which mistakes are much less costly to management than when made through on-the-job trial-and-error means of gaining experience in handling problems of human relations." "Role playing has its foundations firmly in the socio-psychological principle that all human behavior is role playing of some sort and that the essential character of social intelligence involves putting one's self in the place of others." Role playing as well as other action methods of training are imbedded in a democratic concept that there should be consistency between training method, individual, and corporate needs.

Peters, G. A., & Gardner, S. Inducing creative productivity in industrial research scientists. *Group Psychotherapy*, 1959, 12, 178-186.

A special limited-goal program is indicated for research personnel in industry to help individuals develop their creative powers. A *creative-induction* program similar to intensive industrial role playing is indicated, using role playing as a major technique. This program is not concerned so much with personality modifications but rather with the induction of higher levels of creativity.

Peters, G. A., & Phelan, J. G. Practical group psychotherapy reduces supervisors' anxiety. *Personnel Journal*, 1957, 35, 376-378.

The authors contend that many industrial supervisors are in dire need of psychotherapeutic help. One method of meeting this need is to use group psychotherapy in the form of intensive industrial role playing, which is effective in changing the attitudes of supervisors. They claim that "mere familiarity with a new role and experience in handling routine problems associated with new roles lessens the threatening quality of such new social adjustments."

Peters, G. A., & Phelan, J. G. Relieving personality conflicts by a kind of role playing. *Personnel Journal*, 1957, 36, 61-64.

The authors describe intensive industrial role playing, a form of group psychotherapy based on the notion that "knowledge of what is right does not ensure emotional acceptance nor the ability to put knowledge into action." There are four phases to this method: (a) planning, including program orientation, individual interviews, and mapping out procedures; (b) group interaction, including the warm-up, ego involvement, content clarification, and feeling analysis; (c) individual ventilation through periodic interviews, suggested every six sessions; and (d) group interaction in terms of new sequences of six sessions. The authors comment on "the saving in time for the group leader (or lowered costs to industry) in comparison to individual therapy since it . . . requires only 25% as much time . . ." The role-playing leader should provide general direction; his leadership should not be obvious; and he should never place himself in a teaching position.

Peters, G. A., & Phelan, J. G. Practical group psychotherapy and role playing for the industrial supervisor. *Group Psychotherapy*, 1959, 12, 143-147.

A fundamental problem in industry is to determine how to change the basic negative attitudes of industrial supervisors. This is an important problem because there is a direct relationship between the nature of the interpersonal relationships within a company and productivity and profits. *Intensive industrial role playing* offers an economical remedy for improving problems involved in changing basic attitudes of industrial supervisors. Greater responsibility is placed on the group leader in understanding the personality dynamics, assets, limitations, and needs of each individual for good group interaction.

Peters, G. A., & Phelan, J. G. Role playing techniques in industrial situations. *Group Psychotherapy*, 1959, 12, 148-155.

Productivity depends more on psychological than on environmental factors. Psychological factors, to be optimal, depend greatly on proper communication and perceptions, but these depend basically on attitudes. To change attitudes in industry, a type of group psychotherapy using role playing is recommended. The format is that four role players under the direct supervision of a leader interact while four other members serve as observers and commentators. Four phases are identified: (a) planning, (b) group interaction, (c) individual ventilation, and (d) group interaction.

Phelan, J. G. An adaptation of role playing techniques to sales training. *Journal of Retailing*, Winter 1954, 149.

> The best method for training in social skills is to watch others, do it oneself, discuss and evaluate differences, and then try again. Conferences do not permit trainees to get a feeling for how to proceed in a problem situation. Effective sales training using role playing depends on good planning and direction. A discussion is given of general procedures applicable in role playing sales-training and evaluation interviews. The use of role reversal is discussed.

Planty, E.G. Training employees and managers. In E. G. Planty, W. S. Mc-Cord, & C. A. Efferson (Eds.), *Training employees and managers for production and teamwork*. New York: Ronald Press, 1948.

> There sometimes is a discrepancy between apparent understanding and acceptance versus actual behavior on the job. Role playing is a solution because one can project himself in a situation, submit himself for critical evaluation, and practice new procedures and methods. Role playing is the method that evokes the fullest activity in learning. The author distinguishes between role playing in which one acts out a situation spontaneously and a demonstration in which actors show the observers the right and wrong ways to handle human relations problems.

Rubin, C. G. A statement on the practical application of role playing as a selection technique by the Seattle Civil Service Department. *Sociometry*, 1951, 14, 59-62.

> The Seattle Civil Service experimented with role playing for personnel selection and used role playing in selecting policewomen, purchasing agents, and contract agents. These situations, called performance demonstrations, bring out qualities not readily discerned by interviews or written examinations. An example of a structured problem for policewomen is given together with a rating form that includes voice and speech, ability to present ideas, comprehension of problem, judgment, emotional stability, self-confidence, diplomacy, and cooperation.

Scher, J. M. Two disruptions of the communication zone: A discussion of action and role playing techniques. *Group Psychotherapy*, 1959, 12, 127-133.

> Two types of organizational aberrations that result in a disruption of the communicative process within a hierarchical structure are discussed. *Communicatio retarda* is a process that lacks goal-intendedness and results in a situation in which no action is achieved. *Communicatio multiplex* refers to a situation in which too much competing or unorganized information is handled, and is characterized by a lack of leadership and ordered interaction. Both concepts are demonstrated by examples. Role playing is useful in that it keeps the "communication zone" open and ordered. It clarifies the situation and leads to meaningful decision making.

Schinke, S. P., & Rose, S. D. Interpersonal skill training in groups. *Journal of Counseling Psychology*, 1976, 23, 442-448.

> Two group-counseling programs were evaluated—one using behavioral rehearsal and the other using behavioral discussion. Results indicated that both groups showed improvements with significant gains in the rehearsal-contracting condition.

Schmidhauser, H. B. You, too, can role play. *Journal of the American Society of Training Directors*, 1958, *12*(3), 2-11.

Role playing's value in business situations depend on these seven features: (a) others can observe the situation, (b) participants learn by doing, (c) all quickly grasp essential conflicts, (d) conclusions, decisions, and solutions can be arrived at, (e) participation fosters interest and motivation, (f) techniques elicit attitudes, and (g) beneficial cooperation is induced. Eleven terms used in role playing are defined. Some reports of successful use of this procedure are given.

Schmuck, R. A. Helping teachers improve classroom group processes. In W. W. Charters, N. Gage, & M. Miles (Eds.), *Readings in the social psychology of education* (2nd ed.). Boston: Allyn & Bacon, 1969.

Research exploring the relative values of three methods of modifying classroom processes, including role playing, showed that cognitive processes did not change classroom behavior while teacher-development laboratory processes did change both the attitudes of teachers and classroom behavior.

Shaw, M. E. Role reversal: A special application of role playing. *Supervisory Development Today*, 1955.

Role reversal consists of having role players change their positions or parts. It is used for producing insight, as a warm-up device, for developing the situation, and for producing action. Among its various applications are to indicate how to handle grievances and job-instruction training. Examples of the use of role reversal are given together with a generalized procedure.

Shaw, M. E. Role playing—a procedural approach. *Journal of the American Society of Training Directors*, 1956, *10*, 23.

Effective role playing depends on a procedural frame of reference that helps the leader meet ever-changing needs of people in human relations training. Three phases are suggested: (a) the warm-up, (b) the enactment, and (c) post-session analysis. Successful guidance of learning experiences requires that the leader accept the fact that people are capable of solving the majority of their own problems and that a group's experience and understanding are superior to those of any individual, including the leader.

Shaw, M. E. Training executives in action. *Group Psychotherapy*, 1956, *9*, 63-68.

In view of some opinions that role playing might not be acceptable in industrial training, Shaw gives evidence that 79 percent of seventy-three executives who enrolled in a communication course through the American Management Association accepted role playing without special comment. A number of specific comments about this technique are cited.

Shaw, M. E. Organizational considerations in role playing application. *Group Psychotherapy*, 1959, *12*, 156-160.

Role playing in industry thus far has not been utilized to its potential. In most cases it has been used for fairly sterile didactic purposes, concerning itself with "methods," using "canned" situations, and in general not taking advantage of the enormous possibilities inherent in spontaneous role playing as employed in psychodrama. Shaw suggests that industry can use role playing in its more sensitive and powerful sense, especially in the treatment of existing organizational groups in contrast to transient, artificial training groups.

Speroff, B. J. Empathy and role-reversal as factors in industrial harmony. *The Journal of Social Psychology*, 1953, 37, 117-120.

Industrial conflict is provoked or mediated by intercommunication between disputing groups. Empathy serves the role of mediating good communication when defined as "the ability to put yourself in the other person's position." To establish empathy in disputes, when X expresses a point and Y disagrees, Y must present the point himself to X's satisfaction. This is an example of role reversal used to establish empathetic understanding.

Speroff, B. J. The group's role in role playing. *Journal of Industrial Training*, 1953, 7, 17-20.

Good role playing is group centered. It has two major purposes: to allow a person to "feel the role of another" and to permit the player to reveal his true self. A number of specific techniques are described.

Speroff, B. J. Scripts versus role playing. *Personnel Journal*, 1954, 32, 304-306.

Scripts are structured roles that are read by role players. Their main purpose is to give information to the audience. Although for many situations unstructured, spontaneous dramas are superior, for other purposes scripts are better. In deciding which of the two to use, a great many factors have to be taken into consideration.

Speroff, B. J. Rotational role playing used to develop executives. *Personnel Journal*, 1954, 33, 49-50.

The author discusses the value of job rotation and interchange of roles for fuller development of individual executives and for increasing better understanding of the problems of others.

Speroff, B. J. Empathy and role-reversal as factors in communication. *Journal of Social Psychology*, 1955, 41, 163-165.

Role reversal can be used to ensure good communication when ordinary empathetic procedures do not work.

Speroff, B. J. Five uses of sound recordings of a group's role playing. *Personnel Journal*, 1956, 35, 50-51.

Five major uses of sound recordings in industrial role playing are:
1. Recordings of prior sessions can be the basis for a present group's discussion.
2. A session can serve as a model of a good interaction.
3. One can replay a session to have participants rehear what was said.
4. It is possible in this manner to compare different performances.
5. In this manner one can analyze, evaluate, or examine critically any "frozen" session.

Speroff, B. J. The "behind-the-back" way in training conference leaders. *Personnel Journal*, 1957, 35, 411-412, 435.

Speroff suggests the use of the "behind-the-back" technique in the training of industrial-conference leaders. This method calls for the trainee to interact with the group and then retire psychologically by turning his back to the group while they discuss him. This procedure, it is claimed, makes it easier for the group to discuss the "absent" individual, since they are not inhibited by seeing him, and makes easier for him to listen to what is said, since he is not emotionally upset by hearing critical material. Speroff claims that personal insight, empathetic ability, and sensitivity to the feelings of others are developed by this method. More objective self-evaluation and greater skills in personal relations are fostered by this technique.

Speroff, B. J. Group therapy in industry: A case of intragroup conflict. *Group Psychotherapy*, 1957, *10*, 3-9.

The author recounts a case study of a group of industrial employees whose relationships had degenerated progressively. By using a group-therapy approach, including the use of role playing, the relationships were considerably improved in seven weeks.

Speroff, B. J. Role playing versus acting with scripts. *Nursing Outlook*, 1958, *3*, 377-379.

In nursing training, the use of scripts—which are completely structured interchanges intended to show superior ways of dealing with hospital problems—is inferior to the more dynamic procedure of role playing to permit nurses to empathize with other people's feelings.

Speroff, B. J. Group psychotherapy as adjunct training in handling grievances. *Group Psychotherapy*, 1959, *12*, 169-174.

A case history is cited to show how a labor-relations staff was given training by means of a group-therapy-like procedure aimed at improving its functioning. Individual problems were selected, role played, and discussed. First, attention was paid to problems, later, to the individuals. As a result of a number of such sessions, the effectiveness of the supervisors increased, and they were able to handle almost twice as many cases as they had before.

Stahl, G. R. Role playing is ideal for training. *Sales Management*, November 10, 1953, 40.

This article tells how role playing can be used in the training of salesmen. Role playing is useful not only in improving skills but also in changing attitudes. Twenty-four questions are asked and answered about role playing for training.

Stahl, G. R. Training directors evaluate role playing. *Journal of Industrial Training*. 1953, *7*, 21-29.

This is a summary of replies to questionnaires sent in 1951 and 1953 to training directors with reference to role playing in industry. The two major purposes of role playing are to develop skills and to change attitudes. A number of favorable and unfavorable comments sent by training directors are reproduced.

Stahl, G. R. A statistical report of industry's experience with role playing. *Group Psychotherapy*, 1954, *6*, 202-215.

Reports from 107 organizations regarding their reactions to role playing are given. Generally, its two major purposes are to train supervisors and to help people to learn how to deal with specific problems. A number of specific attitudes are discussed in detail.

Stanton, H., Back, C. W., & Litwak, E. Role playing in survey research. *American Journal of Sociology*, 1956, *62*, 172-175.

Survey data obtained through role playing may prove to be better than information obtained through interview procedures. Most subjects can role play; it is not difficult to train administrators to use this technique; and it yields information about the respondent under stress.

Starr, A. Role playing: An efficient technique at a business conference. *Group Psychotherapy*, 1959, *12*, 166-168.

Role playing in a business conference can be an efficient technique for "putting points across." By having people from outside the organization act out conflict situations, those on both sides of an issue can see the others' points of view.

Starr, A. *Rehearsal for living: Psychodrama*. Chicago, IL: Nelson-Hall, 1977.

This text covers the full range of theory and practice of therapeutic role playing.

Steinmetz, C. Recordings help foremen improve industrial relations techniques. *Factory Management and Maintenance*, 1949, *107*, 129-130.

A technique of human relations training using recording as a major method is described. Participants handle a structured case that is recorded. The session is played back later. The major participant has a first chance to list and criticize his performance, then others are permitted to evaluate it.

Stewart, E. C., Danielian, J., & Foster, R. J. Simulating intercultural communication through role-playing. (HumRRO Tech. Rep. 69-7). Alexandria, VA: Human Resources Research Organization.

This report concerns itself with role playing as a means of communicating with individuals of contrasting cultures. Results show that significant exchanges between people of different cultures can be effectively role played and that, as a result, awareness increases for many trainees.

Stivers, S. N., Buchan, L. G., Dettloff, C. R., & Orlich, D. C. Humanism: Capstone of an educated person. *Clearing House*, 1972, *46*, 556-560.

Role playing and human relations training are two important ways to improve the educational processes in the public schools to meet social needs.

Symonds, P. Role playing as a diagnostic procedure in the selection of leaders. *Sociatry*, 1947, *1*, 43-50.

The author analyzes 111 O.S.S. improvisation situations. They fall into seven types: (a) personal criticism (boss criticizes a worker), (b) interpersonal conflict (partnership dissolution), (c) moral issues (plagiarism), (d) interviews (hiring situations), (e) rejection situations (blackballing), (f) intrapersonal conflict (loyalty problems), (g) authority problems (reporting mutiny). These role-playing situations can be used for the evaluation of personality, since different people handle such problems differently.

Taylor, J. W. Methods of increasing knowledge. *Journal of the American Society of Training Directors*, 1953, 7, 13-16.

> Training has three purposes: increasing knowledge, increasing skills, and improving attitudes. There are four ways of increasing knowledge: telling, showing, illustrating, and doing. A dozen ways of increasing knowledge are listed: reading, lectures, etc., including role playing, defined simply as the case-study method brought to life, utilizing the learning-by-doing principle. Role playing permits practice without penalty, allows experimentation, creates new understanding convincingly, and is one of the most potent weapons in the training director's arsenal.

Teahan, J. E. Role playing and group experience to facilitate attitude and value changes among black and white police officers. *Journal of Social Issues*, 1975, 31(1), 35-45.

> Role playing and interpersonal feedback were used in the training of 149 white and thirty-one black police officers with the intention of improving relationships between the black and white officers. Results indicate that while the blacks changed their attitudes towards whites favorably, no changes occurred for the whites, who saw the program as initiated for the benefit of the blacks.

Tupes, E. C., Carp, A., & Borg, W. R. Performance in role playing situations as related to leadership and personality measures. *Sociometry*, 1958, 21, 165-179.

> A test of the hypotheses that role-playing scores (a) are related to military officer effectiveness, (b) are related to other performance predictors, and (c) are related to personality scores rendered by peers. Based on tests of over two hundred USAF candidates, the results indicate that nonchance relationships exist for the first hypothesis but predictions are not efficient; significant relationships exist versus other performance tests; and significant relationships exist between role-playing scores and peer personality ratings. The authors believe that the use of check lists of specific behaviors is a superior method of scoring role playing for evaluation.

Tyler, A. H. A case study of role playing. *Personnel*, 1948, 25, 136-142.

> Role playing was first used in industrial training at the American Type Founders Company. This method has a number of advantages over other procedures, including learning-by-doing; learning is put to immediate use and there is competition to do better than others. Sound recordings and playbacks are a main training tool. Role playing is a difficult task and calls for tact, patience, and understanding on the part of the leader.

Weinland, J. D. Training interviews by the group method. *Journal of the American Society of Training Directors*, 1957, 11(2), 35-40.

> The group training situation has some advantages over individual training for interviewers: criticism occurs without rancor; the group has a wide attention span and observes closely; there is greater freedom for questioning; and individuals are helped to learn how to speak before groups. In the procedure used by the writer, students are interviewed in pairs in front of a class. The instructor also does demonstration interviewing. When special points are to be taken up, planned role playing is used.

Wilkinson, B., & Myers, J. H. What good are role playing techniques? *Advanced Management*, 1954, 19, 23-24.

When role playing is not accepted, it is highly possible that the technique has been misunderstood and/or misused. The authors applied role playing with success in a location where formerly it had not worked out well. They asked one-half the group to identify with one person and the other half to identify with another person in two-person enactions. The players had rehearsed the scene and purposely made errors. The group then discussed these errors. Sixteen questions are asked and answered by the authors.

Wolozin, H. Teaching personnel administration by role playing. *Personnel Journal*, 1948, 27, 107-109.

The author reports that he finds it much more satisfactory to teach personnel administration through role playing. He separates class groups into subgroups of six and has each group analyze and act out problem cases.

Wyn-Jones, I. The significance of role playing. *Bacie Journal*, January-February, 1952, 21-24.

Role playing is defined as "the physical interpretation of a mental pattern of behavior in a given situation." There is reason to doubt whether this procedure has yet been used to its full advantage. Several types of role playing are described: dramatization of training based on a rehearsed script for demonstration purposes (information giving); spontaneous role playing in which students' abilities to handle problems are tested (testing); and role playing for insight through acting in a semistructured situation (training). Post-session analyses are regarded as important. Groups of no more than fifteen members each are suggested for industrial role playing. Success depends in part on the attitudes of the students and the ability of the instructor to create an air of reality about the situation.

Zander, A. F. Role playing: A technique for training a necessarily dominating leader. *Sociatry*, 1947, 1, 225-235.

In some situations, the leader must be dominating and should lead without consideration of the desires of those under his supervision. However, there are a variety of ways in which a necessarily dominating leader can secure better cooperation of subordinates. A condensed description is given of how this type of situation is handled. In a training course that meets for only a few sessions, the use of role playing brings up a number of problems, especially when unsympathetic individuals are in the group.

APPENDIXES

Appendix 1

Case Material

STRUCTURE

In role playing one can distinguish two types of cases: those made up on the spot, which may be called unstructured or developmental, and those prepared in advance, which may be called structured. Structure refers to the relationships that exist among the various elements of the role-play situation. A situation can be structured in various amounts depending on what the facilitator hopes to accomplish. When the facilitator provides instructions or materials with predetermined goals and expectations, the situation is structured. If relationships among people, issues, and other critical factors are defined in detail, the case is highly structured. The less structure there is, the greater is the possibility of variations in individual interpretation. When a role player is told "An employee will come to see you to talk about a problem," very little structure is provided. When also told "You are the personnel officer; among your duties is the supervision of the employees' cafeteria," the role player is given more structure.

FORMAT

Format means the particular procedures used. The situation may be of the "single" kind, with one person role playing before others, or of the "multiple" type, with a number of groups role playing at the same time. The procedure may be straight role playing, or any of the various techniques such as "switching" may be utilized. Ordinarily, the simpler procedures are best, since complicated formats tend to confuse participants. What is important is that the procedure used is appropriate to the group and is useful for the facilitator's intentions.

FOCUS

Any role-play situation has a different meaning or impact for different individuals. Some problems may be of little interest or value to particular people or groups; other situations may evoke intense interest. We can assume generality of needs for any homogeneous group, that is, whatever is meaningful for one individual tends to have meaning for others. The facilitator should be able to understand the needs of the participants and diagnose their individual difficulties. The facilitator will then develop problem situations that are focused on the participants' needs and are meaningful to them.

THE CASES

In the subsequent pages, a number of role-play cases are presented to indicate various kinds of structure, format, and focus. These cases can be used as they are—they have been pretested and found to have general applicability—or the facilitator may wish to modify some of them for special purposes. It is desirable for the facilitator to introduce suitable modifications designed to meet the particular needs of each group worked with.

There is some advantage in a facilitator having a repertoire of familiar cases. In this manner one develops experience with a particular situation, learns how to introduce it to a group, can learn a variety of approaches to the problem, and, most of all, can compare any individual's reactions and solution with those of others.

In order to demonstrate a wide variety of structures, formats, and focuses, the cases differ considerably from each other in these three dimensions; they provide the facilitator with more variations than he or she will ordinarily use. Once secure in the ability to employ a particular format, the facilitator should experiment with new procedures to finally arrive at the point where the needs of any group or individual can be met in a rapid, spontaneous manner.

CASE 1: THE DISSATISFIED EMPLOYEE

Synopsis

This is a specialized approach using an interrupted script. It deals with a manager trying to resolve the dissatisfactions of a subordinate who is about to resign. (Two participants begin by reading a script and then continue working on the problem without the script.)

Goals

1. To warm up participants to a role-play situation.
2. To provide practice in handling conflict, specifically in responding to a dissatisfied employee.

Materials

1. Participant instructions
2. A prepared script

Group Size

Up to thirty people

Time Required

Approximately forty-five minutes

Procedure (Straight or multiple role playing)

1. Identify the objectives of the activity.
2. Describe the process.
3. Solicit volunteers or form teams and have each team select its own pair of role players (handle as a multiple role play). Distribute the participants' instructions.
4. Set time limits.
5. Direct the participants in the role-play enactment.
6. Lead the discussion.

   (Typical discussion topics)
   a. Have you encountered problems like this before?
   b. How does it feel to have to deal with this kind of problem?

   (For role players)
   c. How did you feel about the issue? What are some of the things you would like to try in the future?
   d. What are some factors that contribute to the resolution of this kind of problem?

Participant Instructions

1. You will be asked either to take the role of a manager or a subordinate trying to work out a problem, or you will be asked to observe this process and comment on it later.
2. Two role players will be selected: A is the subordinate; B is the supervisor.

Script

A: Do you want to see me?

B: Yes, please sit down.

A: Thanks.

B: I suppose you know why I called you in?

A: I suppose it is about my resignation.

B: It took me by surprise. I knew you were dissatisfied, but I didn't think you would quit.

A: I discussed it with you.

B: That you were dissatisfied, yes, but I told you I would review your complaints.

A: Look, I told you about the problems six months ago, and you agreed that I had a point. Then I told you about them again three months ago. Once again you told me personally that you would do something about them. Finally, about a month ago, I wrote them out. This week, I still had not heard from you, so I figured you weren't going to do anything and I handed in my resignation.

B: You're justified in quitting. But I hate to lose you. I don't think your resigning is good for you or for us. Now, you came down to three complaints about your job, right?

A: That's right. Just three.

B: Could you tell me them again?

A: What would be the use?

B: Honestly, I have been really busy. Maybe I have a tendency to let things slide, but right now I give you my word that I'll listen carefully and give you immediate action if I think I can do something.

A: They're in my note to you.

B: It's five-thirty and my secretary isn't in. I'll never find them. Do you remember them?

A: Of course I do.

B: Would you be so kind as to tell me what your three complaints are, and then we'll discuss them and I'll give you my answers and solutions.

A: I don't know what this would accomplish.

B: Do you have another job?

A: No, I haven't. But in my field, well—you know as well as I—I won't have trouble getting something.

B: You are a good worker. But if you don't have something else lined up, what can you lose by telling me? And if I can rectify the problems, you'd be satisfied, wouldn't you?

A: I would.

B: Fine. Tell me then, one at a time, and I'll discuss them with you fully, and we'll settle them. If you are dissatisfied, let me know. However, I think we can work this out.

A: O.K.

B: How long do you think this will take?

A: About ten or fifteen minutes, no more.

B. Shoot: what is the first complaint you have about the job?

A: Well, it is . . .

(A and B continue for ten to fifteen minutes.)

CASE 2: HANDLING CUSTOMER OBJECTIONS

Synopsis

This is a sales-training, multiple role-play case. A manufacturer's sales representative must handle the objections of a reluctant retailer. Observers are used to enhance the learning opportunities.

Goals

1. To provide participants with an opportunity to practice handling objections from retail-sales customers.
2. To analyze and improve the sales representative's general communication skills.
3. To aid participants in increasing their understanding of customers.

Materials

1. Participant instructions
2. Observer guides

Group Size

Up to thirty people.

Time Required

One to one and one-half hours

Procedure (Multiple role playing)

1. Briefly describe the general issue: handling customer objections and improving communication. Review approaches and techniques for handling customer objections (ten minutes).
2. Form teams of three to four people each; assign the sales representative role, the retailer role, and the observer(s) role(s). In quartets use two observers.
3. Provide five minutes for participants to read their roles or observer guides. (Participants see only their own assignments.)
4. Have the subgroups begin the enactment. Allow twelve minutes for the role play and ten minutes for feedback and discussion.
5. As appropriate, rotate the roles within each group or rearrange the groups so that others can practice. Again use the twelve-minute, ten-minute time sequence.
6. Review and summarize the subteams' reactions (ten to fifteen minutes).

Participant Instructions

You will be asked to form subgroups of three or four members each. One member of each team will be given the role of the sales representative. A second member will be the customer. The remaining member(s) will be given the observer role.

Instructions for Marion Wilcox

You now own your own retail grocery, after seven years of working for a big chain. Your profits are good, and you are aware that your success depends mostly on your being a smart merchandiser. Every sales representative who comes to see you routinely tries to sell you more merchandise than you can use; and almost every one of them wants you to display the merchandise "up front." They frequently have some gimmick or other. You don't like too many displays because they clutter up the store, but every once in a while, if a display is tastefully done, you do permit one to be set up. Another reason you don't particularly like displays is that you frequently run sales of your own, and you want to push your own special items.

You agreed a week ago to purchase one case of Quickie Instant Orange Juice from the sales representative, Lonnie Rogers. You have decided that it won't hurt to give this brand a try, even though you are already carrying three brands of orange juice. Quickie costs you a penny more per can, and you will have to sell it at two cents more per can to customers. You are told that Quickie makes five instead of four glasses of orange juice, and this is a sales point that will be stressed in television and newspaper ads. So, despite your reluctance to put in a new brand—which causes you more trouble in warehousing—you have decided to try out one case to see how well it sells.

One thing about yourself: you don't like it when sales representatives try to make up your mind for you and tell you what is best for your store. If they know so much, they should be in business for themselves. Right now you have enough free time to talk with Lonnie Rogers, and you want to stay on good terms with this contact, but you are not going to be "sold" something unless you think it is a good proposition.

Instructions for Lonnie Rogers

You are a sales representative for the J.C. Food Company. Your company is putting on a big push for Quickie Instant Orange Juice. Some of its selling points are:

1. Quickie is more concentrated than the competitors' brands. You get almost one full glass more when you buy Quickie. It costs about two cents more per can in the stores, but the consumer saves money on every can.
2. There is strong national advertising support on television and in the newspapers for this new brand. The retail customers will be looking for it.

Your immediate goal is to get your customer to install an attractive point-of-purchase display. The display was scientifically tested in other cities, and increased orange juice sales as much as 30 percent. Marion Wilcox, the store owner whom you will talk to today, already has agreed to purchase one case of Quickie. If the owner accepts the display, you should see whether you can include an additional case in the order, since sales will be more rapid.

Store owners and managers almost always will start out with nominal opposition to your sales pitch, but will permit you to make it.

Instructions for Observers

Read the instructions for Lonnie Rogers and Marion Wilcox. They outline the problem to be enacted. It is your function to note what goes on during the meeting, including positive and negative actions of both role players, but pay special attention to Lonnie Rogers. Check for these points:

1. Rogers' opening remarks. What attitude is conveyed? Is a favorable atmosphere established?
2. Are Wilcox's hidden objections brought out in the open?
3. How does Wilcox respond to Rogers' various points?
4. What techniques does Rogers use to deal with Wilcox's rather reluctant attitude?
5. How well does Rogers present the sales points?
6. What impression does Rogers create on Wilcox?
7. How is the closing of the interview made?

In addition to these points, be ready to comment on any other elements you may notice in the interview.

CASE 3: HANDLING INTERPERSONAL TENSION

Synopsis

This case is designed to explore the feelings associated with dealing with unexpected, awkward, interpersonal situations. The role play ordinarily causes a great deal of tension and anxiety in all participants. It involves three people, each of whom receives instructions to operate in ways that the others do not expect. It is a two-stage problem.

This case is a powerful one for understanding how one of the role players reacts to disappointments and frustrations. It also indicates how well another role player can handle a very unpleasant assignment and how the third deals with a delicate task.

Goals

1. To observe participants in an unexpected situation.
2. To evoke and examine the feelings associated with handling unpleasant interpersonal situations.

Materials

Participant instructions

Group Size

Up to thirty people

Time Required

One hour

Procedure (Multiple role playing)

1. Introduce the role play.
2. Set up multiple role-playing groups, assign the roles, and distribute role instructions.
3. Direct participants to enact the role play.
4. Discuss the results:
   a. What are some of the ways you (the individual group member) deal with unpleasant situations?
   b. What are some of the ways you and others handle frustration?
   c. What are the alternatives that the role players found for coping with the unexpected?

None of the three participants are to know the others' instructions. They should read their parts to themselves or the facilitator should read each role player's part in front of the group while the other two role players are out of the room.

Joe Johnson and Tracy Taft can be seated back to back, but are told that they are in separate offices. Each cannot hear what the other is saying.

Participant Instructions

Instructions for Tracy Taft

You are secretary to Joe Johnson, president of the Johnson Realty Company. Your boss pays well and is very considerate. However, he has his peculiarities. He does not like to be interrupted with calls or visits while he is working, and he likes to have a set schedule. A great many people try to see him, especially salespeople. It is your job to make appointments for these people. At the end of the day you tell Mr. Johnson who came, what they want, and whom they represent, and then he decides if he wants to see them.

Mr. Johnson is especially sensitive about unexpected visitors. They use all kinds of tricks to try to get in to see him.

Today, a person named Lou Phillips will come in to see Mr. Johnson. As usual, you will take the person's name, address, business connection, and purpose of the visit and will make an appointment for the next day, if you can. Phillips probably will be very persistent. Explain your instructions, say that you cannot interrupt Mr. Johnson but that you will let Mr. Johnson know at the end of the day—about 5 p.m. (it is now 2 p.m.)—that Lou Phillips wants to see him. No matter what Phillips' reaction is, after a few minutes go into Mr. Johnson's office and tell him that Lou Phillips is outside. Mr. Johnson will be sitting with his back to you (he is in another office and cannot hear what goes on in your office).

Instructions for Joe Johnson

You are president of the Johnson Realty Company, which was established by your late father. You are an up-and-coming person in this town—a member of the city council, a trustee of the Middletown Country Club—and there is a move to nominate you for mayor. You would be extremely happy to become mayor because there is some talk that you are a success only because your father started the business.

You are in your office. Your secretary sees all visitors and has orders not to disturb you. You like to plan your day and like to have appointments made in advance.

Yesterday, to your surprise, you ran into Lou Phillips, whom you haven't seen for fifteen years. Lou was just about your best friend when you were kids. Your mother didn't like Lou, who was a bit wild in those days and used to get you into all kinds of minor troubles. She used to say, "Lou's too smart in too many ways." But Lou once saved your life when you were swimming in the lake. Yesterday, you learned that Lou is now a marriage counselor and is thinking of coming back and settling down in Middletown. You said, "Drop in to see me at the office."

Last night, at the country club, you mentioned running into Lou Phillips and found out that everybody remembered, and nobody liked, Lou. Some of the people felt that Lou might even be a little crooked. You were surprised at this very negative reaction from so many people.

Lou will probably drop in to see you today. Your problem is to say as tactfully as possible that it would not be a good thing to settle in Middletown. You will tell Lou that there are too many therapists in town now, that the town has changed, and so forth. After all, in view of the attitudes of others, Lou's presence would embarrass you. Be polite but firm. See if you can convince Lou not to move back to Middletown.

Everyone who comes to see you first sees your secretary, Tracy Taft. You will not know that Lou has arrived until your secretary enters your office to tell you. Since Tracy has orders to discourage visitors, maybe Lou will just go away.

Instructions for Lou Phillips

You grew up in Middletown. Fifteen years ago you left to go to college, where you earned a degree in psychology. Ten years ago you married, and you now have two children. You settled down in the big city and became a marriage counselor, and you have done fairly well. However, you always wanted to return to Middletown; it is an ideal place to bring up a family. You are now back in Middletown to look around. This is a good place to live, and you are almost sure that you want to open an office here. There are not many psychologists in town, and you think you could really be successful here.

Yesterday you met Joe Johnson on the street. He was your best friend in high school. He graduated only because you helped him with his math. You and Joe had lots of fun together, and once you saved his life while swimming. You talked only briefly with Joe because you had an appointment at the bank, but Joe did tell you that his father had died and that now he was the head of the Johnson Realty firm. He was cordial to you and asked you to drop in to see him in his office.

Last night you found out that Joe Johnson is now one of the most important people in town. His realty company is the biggest; he is on the city council and is likely to become the next mayor; and he is a trustee of the country club to which all the important people in town belong. There would be no point in your settling down here unless you were a member of the country club. Between that and your friendship with Joe, you could get many referrals for counseling.

Your problem is that it is now 2 p.m. You have another appointment at 3 p.m. You are going to catch a plane at 4:30 back to the city. You are going to go to Joe's office to talk with him and tell him that you have decided to settle down in Middletown.

See if you can get Joe to agree to present your name for membership in the country club. It would be better if you could get Joe to suggest it; if not, bring it up yourself. Get a firm answer one way or another, because unless you can get into the country club, there would be little point in trying to establish a practice in Middletown.

Joe is in his office and cannot hear you while you are talking to his secretary.

CASE 4: STAFF DISAGREEMENTS

Synopsis

This case provides participants with an opportunity to deal with the dynamics of small-group situations. The focus is on "making your point."

This situation is complex, with a good deal of structuring of the attitudes of five people about the autonomy of one of them. Each person's position differs to some extent from that of the others. The problem is to see how well each individual can make his or her point about Jim Rule's autonomy and how well the group as a whole can come up with a good solution to the company's problems.

Each of the role players should be given sufficient time to read and think over the situation. It might be well, if possible, for the role players to study their roles for at least a day.

Goals

1. To increase the participants' ability to deal with divergent opinions.
2. To explore behavior aimed at influencing the opinions of others.
3. To examine attitudes toward personal autonomy.

Materials

Participant instructions

Group Size

Up to fifty people in multiples of five

Time Required

One and one-half hours

Procedure

1. Review the goals of the activity.
2. Divide the participants into groups of at least five members each. Assign roles and distribute role instructions; assign additional members to observe the process and make notes on how divergent views are dealt with.
3. Direct the participants to enact the role play.
4. Lead a discussion of the role play, including group members' experiences in similar situations.

Participant Instructions

Instructions for Jim Rule

You grew up in this town and after finishing high school you went to work as a machine apprentice at the Brown and Green Manufacturing Company. You entered the Air Force and came out four years later. You then graduated from an engineering school and went to work at Brown and Green as a junior engineer. Seven years later you were promoted to head engineer and supervised four other engineers. Three years later when the production chief, Joe Plenty, retired, you got his job—at a salary of almost twice what you made as chief engineer. Not only did you believe that you were the right person for the job, so did everyone else.

However, in the year that you have been production manager, things have not worked out well. First, there were too many accidents and too many rejects. Then there was a flash strike—for no apparent reason. Mostly, there is too much interference. Old Thaddeus Brown, who is president but who really is semiretired, tries to run the plant as he did when there were twenty employees. Now there are four hundred. You resent his going over your head, giving orders in contradiction to yours. Then there is Wally Brown, vice president in charge of personnel and the son of old Mr. Brown. He is meeting-happy and usually calls conferences at the worst possible times. There is a lot of talk, most of it useless. Then there is Sam Green, the son of Samuel Green, one of the original founders. Sam is always interfering with your production. He sells things that you don't have and insists that they have to be made. This interferes with your scheduling. And then there is old Joe Plenty, who was your former boss and retired from your present job. He comes to your office about twice a week, taking up your time with reminiscences. He also talks with the older workers, most of whom are still loyal to him, and keeps them from working. Joe is a member of the board of directors now, so you can't just ask him to leave.

You are pretty disturbed about the situation, and would like to quit. Your wife, who also grew up in this town, will not hear of moving and advises you to learn how to get along better with the others. Actually, you could not find as good a job anywhere else, and if only they would leave you alone, everything would go well.

Today Wally Brown is calling another meeting. His father, old Mr. Brown, has just come back from a six months' vacation in Florida and will be there along with the others. You intend to tell them that you can't do your job unless you have more autonomy. Specifically, this is what you want:

1. Mr. Brown should not give orders over your head. He should give them to you and not to your managers.
2. Wally Brown should schedule regular meetings—one meeting every two weeks would be enough—and not call unscheduled meetings that interfere with everyone's work.

3. Sam Green should discuss new orders with you to see whether you can put them out on time. Many times you have to work yourself and your employees overtime and you still cannot meet the deadlines. This is bad for the workers and the company's image.

4. Joe Plenty should not come into the plant during working hours, at least not anywhere near as often as he does now. He takes up both your time and that of the workers, and they resent it when you indicate that you expect them to stop talking and get back to work. If Joe would restrict his visits to the lunch hour, that would be all right, and he could still see his old friends. If he has anything to say about the business, he should say it at the regularly scheduled meeting of the board of directors.

Instructions for Thaddeus Brown

You are one of the founders of the Brown and Green Manufacturing Company. You are president, but you are semiretired. You have just come back from a six months' stay in Florida, and you are going to attend a meeting of the top men of the company, including your son Wally, who is vice president in charge of personnel, and Sam Green, who is the son of your deceased partner. Sam is now vice president in charge of sales. Also, your old friend Joe Plenty will be there. Joe is a stockholder in the company, formerly was production chief—the job that Jim Rule now has—and is now retired. He is a member of the board of directors and still has an active interest in the company.

You have seen the company go up and down. In the last several years, things have gone well. You have a good team. Your best man is Jim Rule. Jim has been with the company a long time, was formerly chief engineer, and now is production head.

You have been thinking things over, and you have decided that you have been interfering too much with Jim. Also, you know that Joe Plenty has been putting his nose in Jim's business too much. Jim is an excellent engineer, a very ambitious and hard working person with a lot of drive. You wish this were also true of your son Wally, who is filled with a lot of fancy ideas.

It is your intention to say that you will not interfere any longer with Jim Rule's work, and that from now on you want to make major decisions only and not give orders. You also think that Joe Plenty should lay off Jim Rule, who is rather touchy about his authority. Joe has a lot of friends in the shops, some of whom are still loyal to him, and Jim resents this. Sam Green is a kind of playboy, but a good salesman; he doesn't really understand Jim's problems and should coordinate his selling with the factory's potential.

You like Jim Rule, and you think he is the best bet to become president when you retire in a couple of years. You would like to settle some of the frictions in the company as soon as possible. You will lead the meeting with the intention of letting each person have his full say about company problems and then see if you can get everybody to come to a good understanding.

Instructions for Wally Brown

You are the son of Thaddeus Brown, a founder of the Brown and Green Manufacturing Company. Your father is president, and he will probably retire in a year or two. You are vice president in charge of personnel and the most likely candidate to become president when your father retires.

Sam Green, son of your father's deceased partner, is vice president in charge of sales. Sam is a playboy, but a good salesman. He usually is in trouble with Jim Rule, the new production head.

Jim is a good man, an able engineer, but does not know how to get along with people. He is not a very good production man because he is strictly a slide-rule engineer. What he needs is a better understanding of human relations, how to deal more tactfully with people; you think the very best thing for him would be to take a management course. He was a pilot in the Air Force and is really a brilliant engineer, but because of his brusque manners he has created a lot of hostility. The people in the shops don't like him, and it is a good thing that Joe Plenty, the former production head, comes around to smooth things over when there is trouble. There was a flash strike a couple of months ago, and if it weren't for Joe there would have been a general walkout. The men don't like Jim's manners. He also fights with Sam, who tries his best to get orders for the firm.

It is your considered opinion—and you have talked this over with Sam—that Jim ought to take off a couple of months and go to some management school. Joe could take over as production head for the duration.

Jim does not like you very well. He resents the meetings you call, which are mainly intended to help him understand better what he is doing. You think, however, that he is right about one of his complaints: that your father goes over his head too much. As a matter of fact, your father even hires and fires people, which should be your responsibility.

Your major idea at this meeting, which your father will preside over, is that Jim ought to take a course in management and human relations techniques.

Instructions for Sam Green

You are vice president in charge of sales of Brown and Green Manufacturing Company. Your father was one of the founders. He is now dead. Old Thaddeus Brown, the other partner and president, is semiretired. His son, Wally Brown, is vice president in charge of personnel. The organization is run mostly by Wally Brown, Jim Rule, and yourself.

As you see the situation, Jim Rule is just not fit for his job as production head. Sure, he is a good engineer, but he really doesn't know how to deal with people; they become angry because of his manner. He is very tactless with you and just cannot understand that the company depends on orders. No matter how you approach him, he bristles and seems to think that every order is an insult to him.

Joe Plenty, a major stockholder and member of the board, frequently attends your executive meetings. Joe, who was formerly production head, is a wise old man and in your opinion was chiefly responsible for the company's early growth. In your opinion, old Mr. Brown should have retired long ago. He still tries to run the plant as he did forty years ago. Wally Brown is filled with a lot of strange ideas, and is meeting-happy. Old Joe Plenty is a good man, and if you could get another man like him, there would be no trouble with production. You are a good salesman; everybody admits that.

Here is how you size up the situation:

1. Old Mr. Brown ought to retire. Or, at least, he should not interfere with everybody else's jobs.
2. Jim Rule should go back to engineering. He just doesn't have what it takes to be production chief. It would be quite a drop in salary, but the company's interests come first.
3. Joe Plenty should take over production again until a new production chief is hired; or maybe he could come back as advisor and teach Jim Rule how to deal with people better. You have nothing against Jim. You just don't think he is the right person for the job.
4. As far as Wally is concerned, you think he should stick to his personnel work. He isn't much of an asset to the company in any way.

Instructions for Joe Plenty

You were the first employee of the Brown and Green Manufacturing Company, and last year you retired after forty years of service because you felt that the company needed a younger man. You have invested heavily in the company and have about 10 per cent of the shares now, making you the third largest stockholder.

For twenty years you were production head, and when you retired you suggested that Jim Rule succeed you. He is a brilliant, hard working, ambitious person, a bit too stiff and a bit too driving, but he has a good head on his shoulders. You think he will go a long way and is the most likely candidate for the presidency of the firm.

You like Jim, although he is quite sensitive about your coming to the factory. You try as tactfully as you can to give him pointers about running the factory, and you think he really appreciates them although, being young and ambitious, he probably doesn't think he needs them as much as he does. You have calmed down some of the older men who resent him, and it was you who stopped a recent flash strike. You have continually supported Jim. He has had more than his share of bad breaks during the year he has been production head, and old Mr. Brown, the president, took the opportunity this past year to do things he wouldn't have done when you were production head. Also, that young Mr. Wally Brown, old man Brown's son, is full of funny ideas, and he also interferes with Jim. And of course there is Sam Green, the son of the former partner, now head of sales, and he is always trying to make trouble for Jim.

Old Mr. Brown is back from his vacation (which you suggested, by the way) to discuss giving Jim some freedom. Wally has called another meeting, which you shall attend.

Here is how you size up the situation:
1. Jim Rule is a good man, and the others should lay off him.
2. Thaddeus Brown ought to think of retiring soon.
3. Wally Brown ought to mind his own business and just hire and fire people.
4. Sam Green should be considerate of Jim in writing orders and he should have an understanding of Jim's problems. After all now, with unions and all kinds of government restrictions, one can't be as flexible as one could in the old days.

Thaddeus Brown will run the meeting, and your usual procedure is to shut up and listen, and when everybody else is pretty run down, you give your ideas and make your suggestions.

CASE 5: REVEALING YOURSELF

Synopsis

There are a few training and assessment situations in which an unexpected problem or confrontation is presented to a participant. In dealing with the unexpected, participants learn more about themselves and each other.

Goals

1. To develop spontaneity and an experimental climate.
2. To provide participants with an opportunity to learn more about each other.

Group Size

Up to thirty people

Time Required

Thirty minutes

Procedure

1. Present the background instructions to the group.
2. Conduct the role-play conversations with group members.
3. Discuss the members' reactions and insights.

   (Typical discussion topics)
   a. What do you feel is unique and important about yourself?
   b. What did you observe in this situation that you identified with?
4. Have other members explore how they present themselves in new situations.
5. Use these incidents to lead to discussions or role-play cases regarding openness, trust, and communication in:
   a. employment interviews,
   b. performance discussions,
   c. interpersonal relations.

This situation is unique in that participants receive no role instructions. The situation demonstrates the participant's ability to summarize succinctly and clearly his or her thoughts about self. It is quite revealing, and no group member should be forced to participate. One member participates at a time.

The participant is told, "You are at home alone. It is a Sunday evening. The telephone will ring and you will answer it. Imagine that the telephone is at your elbow. You will receive all other information over the telephone."

The facilitator or an assistant makes a ringing sound to simulate a telephone bell, and then reads off the script that follows. (A disconnected or toy telephone will lend realism to the enactment.)

Instructions for Facilitator

Make a sound like a telephone ringing. The participant will answer the telephone. Then you say (slowly and distinctly), "This is Undersecretary of State Harold McAbee calling from the State Department in Washington, D.C. You have been suggested for an assignment of considerable importance to the welfare of this country. I cannot yet tell you the nature of this matter, but I do need some information about you." (Pause.) "Are you willing to give it to me?" (Pause.)

If the participant says "Yes," go on to the prepared script that follows. If he or she hesitates, inform the participant that the question you wish to ask will be of a personal, but very general nature. When the participant agrees, continue:

"Before I ask you this question, let me tell you that this is sort of a test, designed to see how well you answer questions. Our conversation is being recorded, and you will have exactly five minutes to answer. I cannot repeat or discuss the question. Are you ready?" After receiving assent say, "This is the question: tell me all about yourself in five minutes; about your personal history, educational history, social history, and employment history. I will tell you when the five minutes are up. Do not begin until I say 'Now'." Wait ten full seconds and then say, "Now!" Keep time, and at the end of five minutes say, "Thank you, we appreciate your cooperation. We will review your information and will notify you of our selection soon."

CASE 6: MAKING YOUR POINT/GROUP PROBLEM SOLVING

Synopsis

This case combines group problem solving with face-to-face interviewing. It is a complicated role play, with four separate scenes: the president reads off a statement to a consultant; the consultant has an interview with the manager, who relays certain information; the consultant then meets with the manager and the workers; and lastly, the consultant meets again with the president to report.

Each of the seven people in the situation have separate instructions. While the major purpose of this role play is to test the consultant's capacity to find a proper solution to the problem (there are a number of possible solutions) it is no less a test of the other individuals who are to present their points of view as plausibly as possible.

Goals

1. To improve communication skills between individuals and within a group.
2. To provide an opportunity for group interaction and practice in dealing with conflict.

Materials

Participant instructions

Group Size

Up to fifteen people

Time Required

One and one-half hours

Procedure

1. Identify the goals of the role play and give general instructions.
2. Assign roles, outline the procedure, and distribute role instructions.
3. Have participants enact the role play. When the discussion between the consultant and the workers has been going on for a few minutes, direct the participant who is playing Ronnie Meyer to join the group.
4. Discuss the enactment, including topics such as:
   a. What helps or hinders clear exchange of information?
   b. What steps and processes contribute to problem solving in small groups?

Observer guides and check lists can be used to focus on key issues.

Participant Instructions

Instructions for Henry Raymond

You are a very busy president of an industrial firm. An industrial consultant whom you have never met is coming to see you. You will give the consultant no more than three minutes of your time. You don't know the consultant's name and don't care to know it. Simply tell the consultant that there is a problem going on at the plant. You want the consultant to meet Michael Sanderson, the manager, who will describe the problem. You want the consultant to talk over the problem with the manager and the workers, come up with a solution, and report back to you with the manager. After you have told the consultant this, call in Michael Sanderson, introduce them to each other, and leave.

Instructions for the Consultant

You have been called in by Mr. Henry Raymond, the president of an industrial firm, to act as a consultant for a problem in the company's plant. You have never met Mr. Raymond and have never been in the plant before. This is what will happen to you:

1. You will meet the president, who will tell you something about the problem.
2. You will be introduced to the manager, Michael Sanderson, whose workers are causing the trouble, and you will try to get more information.
3. The manager will introduce you to the workers, and you will get further information. You will try to work out a solution to the problem. You will try to obtain agreement from everybody that the solution is a good one.
4. You will then return with the manager to report to the president, and you will present your recommended solution.

Instructions for Michael Sanderson

You are the manager of an industrial plant. You have been having a lot of trouble with one group of employees about a particular problem. The president, Henry Raymond, has hired a consultant to solve the problem. When the president introduces you to the consultant, don't reveal what the problem is. Tell the consultant that you think the workers should describe the problem, since you don't want to influence the case in any way. Be very firm about this. You have never met this consultant before.

Take the consultant to the workers, introduce them, and try to keep out of the discussion as much as possible. Agree with the workers as much as you can. When the discussion is over and the consultant goes back to the president, go along as the president has directed you, and when the consultant proposes a solution to the problem, try to knock as many holes in it as you can.

Instructions for Lee Baker

You work with Mickey McKelvie, Fran Schutz, and Ronnie Meyer. Ronnie is not in today. There has been a lot of trouble in your department, and the manager, Michael Sanderson, has not been able to solve the problem. You understand that the company is going to hire a consultant to reach a solution. You will try to tell the consultant in front of the manager and the other workers just how you see things and what the right answer should be.

You are the first in the production process. The work comes to you and you set it up so that Mickey McKelvie can work on it. You have to go with your hand truck to another department to get the materials, and frequently there are only one or two pieces. When this happens it means you have to make a lot of trips. If Ronnie Meyer at the other department would have full loads for you, you wouldn't have to make so many trips, since you can easily carry twenty pieces at a time. You think the other department should keep a stockpile and keep ahead of you. You have other things to do, such as packing final items and keeping the workroom clean, and you don't think it is right that you have to keep running back and forth all the time with one or two pieces. Mickey gets pretty angry when you don't have any work ready. As you see it, it is the manager's fault that Ronnie doesn't have enough pieces to keep ahead of you.

Instructions for Mickey McKelvie

You work on piecework. The work is brought to you by Lee Baker, who is supposed to keep you supplied. Whenever you ask for more materials, Lee grumbles and tells you to wait a while. Lee has a lot of other things to do and hates to go to the other department to Ronnie Meyer for the materials unless there is enough for a full hand truck. Sometimes you have gone yourself to get the materials, and you have found more than a truckfull. The other department is also run by your manager, Michael Sanderson. Ronnie Meyer is off on sick leave today. You think that if Ronnie could signal Lee whenever there is enough work for you, there would be no trouble.

Another fellow who gives you trouble is Fran Schutz. Supposedly the chips from your work fly about and sometimes get in Fran's eyes. This is true, but you can't help it. The room you work in is small, and you work face to face with Fran. When you are working you can't always be careful. Fran ought to wear glasses or something.

Instructions for Fran Schutz

You work on piecework. Your co-workers include Lee Baker and Mickey McKelvie. Mickey works immediately adjacent to you, and Lee brings work and materials from another department (from Ronnie Meyer). Mickey and Lee always seem to be bickering about something and, as far as you are concerned, they are so busy worrying about "who's supposed to do what" that they don't pay sufficient attention to their own jobs.

Mickey McKelvie, in particular, does not use proper precautions and permits chips to scatter. On several occasions small chips have flown into your eye. You have spoken to Lee Baker about this, but Lee never seems willing to do anything.

Every once in a while someone calls small groups of workers together to talk about problems. There have not been any discussions lately, but if there is another opportunity, you plan to talk about housekeeping and carelessness on the job. You are really tired of McKelvie's lack of consideration. You hope there will be a meeting some time soon with your foreman, Michael Sanderson.

Instructions for Ronnie Meyer

You came in late to work today because you weren't feeling well, but you received a call telling you that a consultant is coming into the shop to discuss a problem that affects you. You do work on some objects, and when you finish them, you put them down. Then Lee Baker comes and takes them to another room where Mickey McKelvie works on them. Sometimes you pile up a lot of work, and Lee does not come, and you have no place to put the materials, so you have to take Lee's hand truck and take the work to Mickey yourself. Sometimes when Lee comes there are no pieces, or only a couple, and Lee gets angry about having made the trip. If you had more space so you could keep about one hundred pieces waiting, it would solve the problem, and you could keep well ahead of Lee. Also, if there were some way to let Lee know when you are ready, it would help.

(You will enter the room when the facilitator gives you a signal. Your foreman's name is Michael Sanderson.)

CASE 7: REACHING AGREEMENT

Synopsis

This case provides rapid entry into group-problem-solving processes.

Goals

1. To practice group problem solving.
2. To examine processes for reaching agreement.

Materials

Participant instructions

Group Size

Up to thirty people

Time Required

One hour

Procedure

1. Introduce the role play as a group-problem-solving activity and ask for five volunteers or, if the group is large, form multiple sets of five role players each. One or more observers may be assigned to each group of role players.
2. Role players in each group are assigned the roles of Tony Black, Terry Black, Gerry Sims, Rene Johns, and Pat Carey.
3. Distribute the role-play background story to each participant and read it aloud, making sure that each role player understands the problem.
4. Tell role players to begin the staff meeting. After fifteen or twenty minutes, tell the role players that they have five minutes more in which to reach a decision. After five minutes, end the role play.
5. Have observers report on the group behavior of each individual, the group process, and the decisions reached. If two or more groups role played, try to discover why the groups' decisions may have been different.

   (Sample Discussion Questions)

   a. What feelings and reactions did role players experience when others resisted their ideas?
   b. How can group members share and utilize information to arrive at a conclusion?

   (Discussion option: Force field analysis)

   c. Identify factors that contributed to resolution of the issues (helping forces).

    d. Identify factors that made it difficult to reach agreement (hindering forces).

    e. Point out three options for facilitating change: reducing or eliminating hindering forces; adding new, positive forces; or combining the two previous steps.

    f. Discuss ways of accomplishing the options for facilitating change (identify goals clearly; avoid win-lose positions—search for alternatives; gather data before pushing for solutions; and explore the views of others).

Participant Instructions

The Acme Manufacturing Company has a staff meeting the last Tuesday of every month. Today the following five people will be present: Tony and Terry Black, who are co-owners of the Acme Manufacturing Company, Gerry Sims, the production manager, Rene Johns, the sales manager, and Pat Carey, the personnel and training director. Tony is the senior partner and will run the meeting. Tony has no vote in any decision but does contribute opinions.

Terry Black, who is retired, believes that training is a waste of time, and that Pat Carey's assistant, who spends all his time doing training, should be fired or spend his time doing personnel work. Terry feels that the company, which has two hundred employees, does not need a training program.

Gerry Sims, who is the production manager, wants to become a vice president. Gerry has spent eighteen years with the company and believes that the training program is valuable and has paid off in higher production and fewer accidents. Gerry also thinks that Rene Johns, the sales manager, should check with production before accepting any new contracts and should not agree to supply special orders.

Rene Johns also wishes to become a vice president, in charge of sales. Rene has no opinion about training but does think that Pat Carey should do a better job of recruiting personnel, especially a better quality of salespeople. Rene is convinced that expansion of the company depends on sales and that any special services pay off in the long run.

Pat Carey has been offered a new job with a larger salary but would accept a 10 percent raise, which would be equivalent to the new salary. Pat is in urgent need of a secretary in addition to the training assistant, who has been doing an excellent job. If the assistant is fired, Pat will resign.

All five of these people have discussed these issues in the past. Tony Black is quite eager that some satisfactory decisions be made today.

CASE 8: TAPPING GROUP RESOURCES

Synopsis

This case represents a common business problem: a supervisor has to make decisions that affect a number of people and, in order to reach the most equitable solution, meets with the individuals to determine the most satisfactory compromise.

Goals

1. To practice group problem-solving skills.
2. To provide participants with practice in observing and critiquing group processes.

Materials

Separate instructions for each participant

Group Size

Up to forty people (no less than fourteen)

Time Required

One and one-half hours

Procedure

1. Introduce the role play, assign the seven roles, and tell additional members that they will serve as observers. If the group is large, multiple role playing can be used.
2. Assign observers to examine and report on the behavior of specific role players. If a number of groups work on the problem (multiple role playing), one observer can be assigned to each group, to report on all members.
3. Separate instructions for each role player and observer should be prepared. These are distributed to the appropriate members so that each person understands only his or her own situation.
4. Provide ten to twenty minutes for the role play.
5. Ask the observers to report their observations. In the evaluation, the behavior of the supervisor is most important. Another item to look for is the efficiency of the problem-solving group, as noted in the instructions for observers.
6. Reconvene the total group and discuss general findings.

Participant Materials

Instructions for Jean

You are a supervisor, with six people working under you: Al, Lynn, Gale, Jan, Ronnie, and Francis.

1. Al is sixty-two years old and has been with the company fifteen years.
2. Lynn is forty-five years old and has been with the company twenty years.
3. Gale is forty years old and has been with the company seventeen years.
4. Jan is thirty-eight years old and has been with the company twenty years.
5. Ronnie is thirty-five years old and has been with the company two years.
6. Francis is twenty-nine years old and has been with the company eight years.

Yesterday you received a note from your personnel director; it reads as follows:

Dear Jean:

   Vacations this year will be in the months of July, August, and September. Each of the six employees you supervise is to have two weeks vacation, preferably on consecutive weeks to prevent payroll trouble. Do not schedule more than one person out at any time, so as not to affect production schedules. Send me your list of employees and their vacation dates as soon as possible. I suggest that you discuss this with the entire group to arrive at the best possible schedule with the least amount of difficulty.

This is the first time you have discussed vacations with this group. You have to make the scheduling decisions today. Of course you will try to find the best solution.

Instructions for Al

You are sixty-two years old and have been with the company for fifteen years.

For more than thirty years you have vacationed at a summer camp during the first two weeks in July. You have always met with your friends and family at the camp. Last year, because of scheduling problems for vacations, you went the second and third weeks in July, which you did not like at all. You have strict orders from your wife to fight for your rights and to take your vacation the first two weeks in July. If this is not possible, the second and third weeks are acceptable. You already have rented your cabin at the lake, and if you have to change your vacation, you may lose your deposit.

You are the oldest person in your work group, but you have only fifteen years of seniority. Only Ronnie and Francis have less seniority than you.

Instructions for Lynn

You are forty-five years old and have twenty years of seniority. Only Al is older than you, and only Jan has as much seniority as you.

You would prefer to take your vacation the first two weeks in July because they usually are the hottest weeks of the summer. However, if others want this period badly, you are willing to take the second two weeks in July.

Instructions for Gale

You are forty years old, and have been with the company for seventeen years. Al and Lynn are older than you, and only Lynn and Jan have more seniority.

You would like to take your vacation in July, especially the second two weeks. Otherwise you want the first two weeks in August. You would even take the last two weeks in August, but September is out because you have children who have to be back in school in September.

Instructions for Jan

You are thirty-eight years old and have twenty years of seniority in the company. If vacations come up, you feel that you and Lynn have first and equal say, since you both have the same amount of seniority.

Your in-laws are going to stay with you the first two weeks in July, so you will *not* want that period. You have school-aged children so you do not want to take your vacation in September. It would be all right with you to take the last two weeks in July or possibly any two weeks in August.

Instructions for Ronnie

You are thirty-five years old and have only two years of seniority, less than anyone else in your work group.

You already have made plans to go to a summer hotel during the first two weeks in September, when the rates are lower.

Instructions for Francis

You are twenty-nine years old and are the youngest worker in your group, but you have eight years of seniority. Ronnie and Al have less seniority than you.

You would like to have your vacation in July, but would settle for the first two weeks in August. If you have to take your vacation in September, you will not be able to go away unless you can get the first two weeks, because school for your two kids starts on September 15.

Instructions for Observer

Your main task is to observe the individual assigned to you: it may be Jean, the supervisor, whose problem is to set up a vacation schedule, or any one of the six workers who will be affected by the schedule.

If you are assigned to observe the whole group, notice the things each person does, writing down any comments you have. The supervisor's task is to arrive at a quick, reasonable, sensible, peaceful solution. Each of the other individuals have certain demands. Note how they respond to the decisions made.

CASE 9: INCREASING SELF-AWARENESS/ DISCIPLINING OTHERS

Synopsis

This is a relatively unstructured situation designed to increase both self-awareness and sensitivity to others. It deals specifically with discipline about tardiness.

Goals

1. To increase awareness of the two levels of communication that occur in interpersonal situations: what people are saying and what they are feeling.
2. To learn more about the dynamics of disciplinary situations.

Materials

Participant instructions

Group Size

Up to thirty people

Time Required

One hour

Procedure (Straight role playing)

1. Introduce the role play as a somewhat complicated case utilizing two participants—a new employee and a supervisor—and their inner selves.
2. Discuss:
   a. The two levels of communication, as stated in goal 1.
   b. The need to understand the inner feelings and motives of others.
3. Obtain four volunteers. Designate two of them as A and B and tell them to go to the front of the room. Then tell them that their "inner selves" will clarify the situation. Designate the two other participants as A and B's inner selves and give them each the appropriate script for the character (A or B) only.
4. Tell the other group members that they are to serve as observers. They can be broken into two groups, one group to observe A and the other to observe B.
5. Direct the inner self for B to take B out of the room, as indicated in the instructions. Allow the inner self for A time to read his or her instructions and then direct A's inner self to begin. (After reading A's background material, A's inner self will take A out of the room and B's inner self will return with B.)

6. When B's inner self has read B's background material aloud, call A and A's inner self back into the room and tell A and B to begin to role play.
7. Allow the role play to continue for ten to fifteen minutes and then call time. Ask the observers to report on what they observed.
8. Lead a group discussion of the words used versus the feelings of the role players and how this affected the disciplinary situation and vice versa.

Participant Instructions

Instructions for A's Inner Self

You are the "inner self" of A. Stand behind A and read the background material in the following paragraphs to A. Read slowly and clearly. After you finish reading, leave the room and take A with you. When you leave the room tell B's inner self only to bring B into the room. The facilitator later will ask both you and A to come back. While you are out of the room, tell A that when you return, you will join the other group members in watching A and B act out the situation.

My name is A, and I am a manager. I have been a manager for six months, and I am anxious to do a good job.

Yesterday my boss called me in. "A," he said, "Too many employees are late for work, and too many people stay out too long on coffee breaks. I want you to run a tight shop here. It is your responsibility to make sure that people come in on time and give the company the time they are being paid for. I want you to talk to them, especially the new workers like B. B has been around for only about two weeks and already is coming in late. Can you talk to B and straighten things out?"

I told my boss, "Sure, but you know that many of the older employees come in late. They have been doing it for a long time, and I think we should start with them." But the boss insisted that I talk to B first.

I don't like this situation. I think what is right for one is right for all. But this is my job, and I have to do what I am told to do. So this morning I came in before 8:30, which is the company's starting time. Sure enough, B was not in yet. I left a note on B's time card telling B to come see me right away. It is a quarter to nine already, and B is not in yet. I am now in my office, and when B comes in, I am going to put it on the line. I will say as nicely but as firmly as possible that B must come in on time and that is all there is to it. It is now 8:46 and I am still waiting.

Leave the room and take A with you.

Instructions for B's Inner Self

You are the "inner self" of B. As soon as you receive these instructions, you will take B and leave the room. Finish reading these instructions while you are out of the main room. Both you and B will return to the room when A and A's inner self leave it. When you are back in the room you will read the following background material aloud to B. You will stand behind B, and you will read very slowly and very distinctly. When you finish reading, you will sit down. Tell B that when you return to the room, you will provide B's role instructions and then B and A will role play.

My name is B. I just started working in this company two weeks ago. My boss is A and is a pretty nice person. I have just punched my time card and I see a note on it from A. It reads, "Come in to see me as soon as you arrive." I wonder what A wants? What is it all about? I don't like this; it feels like trouble!

My card reads 8:43 a.m. I am thirteen minutes late; can this be the reason A wants to see me? No one else comes in on time. Everybody punches in late. There is Gene punching in right now, and there is Sal coming in through the door, so it can't be that; everybody told me when I started coming in on time that no one came in before a quarter to nine. I'm only doing what the others are doing. I don't want them to think I am trying to be better than anyone else. And besides, sometimes I stay later than the others. All you have to do is look at my time card and you can see that I average more than eight hours a day.

This is a pretty good job. I like it. The other employees are fine and so is A. I will go and wash my hands and then I will go into A's office and see what this is all about. Oh, here comes A now. (Loud and clear:) "Hello, A, I was just coming in to see you."

Sit down with the other observers.

CASE 10: INCREASING ROLE FLEXIBILITY

Synopsis

This is an unusual case aimed at increasing insight, spontaneity, and flexibility. It focuses on resolving interpersonal conflict. Two techniques are used in this case: role reversal and the chain.

Goals

1. To practice resolving conflict.
2. To develop role flexibility.
3. To develop insight into how others feel in a conflict situation.

Materials

Facilitator instructions

Group Size

Up to twenty-four people (an even number is preferable)

Time Required

One to two hours

Procedure

1. Introduce the role play, select role players, and direct the enactment, using the facilitator instructions as a guide.
2. At the conclusion of the last enactment, have the group members discuss what they learned from the activity.

Facilitator Instructions

Follow this script in directing the role play. Be clear and emphatic, but try to avoid talking too much or being too bossy.

Today we are going to experiment with two different role-playing techniques. The first one is a role-reversal in which two characters, named Courtney and Dale, face a situation that I will describe in a moment. Then Courtney and Dale will reverse roles, that is, Courtney will play the role of Dale and Dale will assume the role of Courtney, continuing from the point at which I stopped them. This technique has the advantage of helping the role players understand each other's roles.

After that, we will use the chain technique, which is something like role reversal except that we will obtain different role players from the group. We may see a number of people playing each role.

This session should be a lot of fun but can be confusing, so I will start and stop the action several times. The role players will please follow my signals.

Now, here is the problem. Dale is Courtney's work supervisor. Courtney wants to convince Dale, the boss, of something. Dale is resistant. So the problem is for Courtney to try to convince Dale, who, on the other hand, wants to convince Courtney. We now have the classic requirements for a conflict. Let us see how Courtney and Dale can work out the problem. This is it:

Courtney drives a truck for a living and is dissatisfied with the truck. We will find out why from whomever plays Courtney. Dale understands Courtney's point of view but also knows that the company will not issue Courtney a new truck.

The setting is Dale's office. Dale will be seated here and Courtney will come in. Courtney may be in a good mood and may want to discuss the issue or may be pretty angry about the truck and make a big issue out of it; this is up to Courtney. The same can be said about Dale, who may be relaxed and happy to talk to Courtney, may be busy, or may get angry. Again this will be up to Dale.

At this point, divide the members into two groups: one group to be Courtney and the other to be Dale. Direct the groups to opposite sides of the room and pick two members from each group. Announce that one Dale and one Courtney will leave the room while the other pair role plays so that ways of dealing with the situation can be compared. When one pair leaves, direct the other pair to begin the first role play.

Dale will be seated in the office. When I give the signal, Courtney will enter and begin. Remember, it is Courtney's problem to talk Dale into getting a new truck. Courtney may come up with as many reasons as possible for this need or may simply stick to one or two good arguments.

Everyone else should observe how Courtney and Dale act. Many of you will have a chance to play the roles today; you will all have a chance to learn from others alternative ways of resolving conflict. Try not to laugh or interrupt the role play. For those of you who are role players, when I clap my hands twice, stop role playing immediately and wait for further instructions. All right Courtney, go into see Dale.

Let the situation go on about three to five minutes, then clap your hands twice. Ask the role players to rejoin their groups and call in the second pair of role players. Give them the same instructions you gave the first role players, and direct them to begin the enactment. When Courtney and Dale seem to be interacting strongly—two or three minutes—clap your hands and tell the role players to exchange roles and continue their discussion where it left off. Let them continue from this point for about two minutes, then clap your hands and *gesture* to indicate that they should exchange roles again and continue. *Say nothing.* In this way you train the members to obey signals. Let them continue about one minute, then clap your hands once again and signal another change. Let the scene continue about a minute or so, then clap your hands again and tell the role players to sit down.

At this point you may lead the group in a discussion of the two different role plays. During the discussion, *you should give no opinions.* This is important.

After the discussion, say:

Now, we will use the chain technique. Those members in each role group who have not yet been on the stage will count off—1, 2, 3, etc. Courtney 1 and Dale 1 will begin the role play from when Courtney enters Dale's office. When I clap my hands, the role players will stop talking. Then I will point to Courtney 2, and he will take Courtney 1's place and continue the conversation with Dale 1. After a while I will clap my hands again and point to Dale 2. In this way you all will have a chance to participate. Now, Courtney 1 and Dale 1; begin the conversation.

Permit the first interaction to continue for two or three minutes, then clap your hands and have Courtney 2 replace Courtney 1. After another minute or so, clap your hands again, and motion to Dale 2 to replace Dale 1. Continue until every member has had a chance to participate.

At the end of the role plays, reassemble the group and ask members what they learned from the activity.

Appendix 2

Observer Guides

ROLE-PLAY OBSERVER GUIDES: ONE-ON-ONE

Many role plays involve one-on-one communication situations such as sales situations, counseling, performance review, fund raising, and teaching or training. These situations usually involve one or more of the following issues or functions:

1. Setting a goal
2. Solving a problem
3. Selling a product or idea
4. Resolving conflict
5. Providing support or guidance
6. Determining a course of action.

Since everyone deals with such issues at one time or another many role plays focus on one or more of these topics.

With appropriate modification, the observer guides that follow can be used for a wide range of role plays.

Guide 1: Force Field

Instructions: During this interview (sale, disagreement, counseling situation) two basic kinds of behavior occurred:

1. Behavior that contributed to progress or forward movement (reaching agreement, resolving differences, clarifying issues, or developing a course of action).
2. Behavior that hindered forward movement.

Note any examples of the first kind of behavior (helping or problem-solving behavior) in the first column on the following chart. Examples: clarifying purpose, asking questions, avoiding win-lose behavior, etc. Then note examples of distracting or hindering behavior in the second column. Examples: failure to listen or explore, taking a dogmatic position, etc. After the role play is complete, discuss your observations and recommendations with the entire group.

Force Field Format

Helping, Problem-Solving Behavior (give examples)	*Distracting or Hindering Behavior* (give examples)
1.	1.
2.	2.
3.	3.
4.	4.

1. What could be done to reduce hindering behavior?

2. What could be done to increase helping behavior?

3. Other comments:

Guide 2: Giving and Seeking Information

Instructions: When two people are engaged in a discussion, one or both must give information: facts, experiences, feelings. One or both also must seek information by asking questions, challenging others, or exploring feelings and opinions. Note on the following check list the kinds of information-seeking and information-giving that take place in the face-to-face situation you are observing. You are asked to observe (name of role player).

The person I observed

Gave information by:

(Rank: 1-not enough; 2-about right;
            3-too much)

1. Providing facts without
   pressure   _____

2. Taking a strong and
   positive position   _____

3. Pointing out the pitfalls of a
   given course of action   _____

4. Becoming enthusiastic   _____

5. Indicating the benefits of
   his or her points   _____

6. Suggesting alternatives   _____

7. Other

Sought information by:

(Rank: 1-not enough; 2-about right;
            3-too much)

1. Asking direct questions   _____

2. Asking open-ended dis-
   cussion questions   _____

3. Demonstrating interest
   and concern   _____

4. Rephrasing or summa-
   rizing the other's point
   of view   _____

5. Exploring the potentials
   of the other's position   _____

6. Explaining alternatives   _____

7. Other

Comments:

Comments:

ROLE-PLAY OBSERVER GUIDES: GROUP INTERACTION

In every group situation, people must reach agreement, solve problems, or make decisions. Several of the role-play cases outlined previously deal with group interaction. The observer guides that follow can be adapted for use with these and other cases.

Guide 1: Group Interaction

Instructions: You will be asked to observe one or more of the functions on the following check list. Next to each function a space is provided for your comments or observations. (Optional: a space is provided to write in the names of group members who perform these functions.)

Group Functions

Function	Brief Example	Performed By

Establishing and maintaining direction

_____ Setting or clarifying goals

_____ Summarizing progress

_____ Testing for agreement

Dealing with disagreement

_____ Seeking diverse viewpoints

_____ Clarifying or reconciling opposing views

_____ Suggesting alternatives

Providing systematic procedures

_____ Providing frameworks (recording), suggestions, orderly procedures

_____ Developing criteria for making judgments

_____ Establishing priorities (avoiding trivia, sidetracks)

Providing support and openness

_____ Listening to and exploring other's views

_____ Showing understanding (even for
unpopular positions)
_____ Showing respect for individuals
_____ Expressing feelings and ideas with
candor

Developing conclusions/Courses of action
_____ Summarizing progress
_____ Weighing alternatives
_____ Suggesting action or follow-up

Guide 2: Group Interaction

Instructions: The effectiveness of a group discussion is often enhanced when resources within the group are tapped. The following is a list of group and individual resources. Check any of the resources you observe in the group and make brief notes about how (or if) each resource was drawn out and used.

Resource	*Used To* (Or Not Used To)	*Drawn Out By* (Or Ignored By)
_____ Knowledge of the issue		
_____ Knowledge of group processes		
_____ Capacity to analyze		
_____ Capacity to operate systematically		
_____ Capacity to build on ideas		
_____ Personal energy, enthusiasm		
_____ Capacity to collaborate		
_____ Diverse experience		
_____ Diverse feelings		
_____ Capacity to reach awareness		
_____ Capacity to act		

Comments:

Appendix 3

Role-Player Rating Sheets

When a group meets for a number of sessions for training purposes, a rating sheet can be helpful. Such a sheet can be used to inform any individual about the opinions of others and also can serve as a guide for discussion. The sheet illustrated in this section represents a "universal" rating system that can be employed for many purposes. By modifying terms, one can make this sheet more specifically useful for any particular group.

The "Directions" contain instructions that are sufficient for trainees. The reason for using the unusual format of a circle and an underline is because frequently no one can tell which of any two different behaviors is better. For example, we cannot say whether it is better to be firm or to be flexible; the answer depends on the situation. Therefore, by means of the circle and underline technique, the rater can indicate what he or she thinks is right (by underlining) and what he or she saw (by circling) during the role play. The difference between the two ratings is the "error"—the disparity between what was observed and what was deemed correct.

After ratings are made, and after a group discussion, the forms are given to the role-play protagonist. By looking over the ratings for the specific factors, by comparing the opinions of the members, and by reading any comments the raters may have made on the back of the sheets, the protagonist receives feedback material.

The information on these sheets can be transferred to the "Role-Player Summary Chart" that follows the rating sheets. On the sample chart are drawn a variety of curves to show some possible patterns. The curve for "stand" is rather flat, indicating little change from session to session; but for "control" we see a rapid change for the better. This individual, who averaged about "5" in the first session, has moved up to "1½" by the tenth session (the lower the score the better). The curve for "communication" is high overall with some variations. A person reading this would be told that this is an area in which he or she does well. For "attitude" we see little change over the first four sessions and then a rapid rise, sustained over the next several sessions. For "emphasis" we see a slow and gradual change. In terms of "relations," however, the curve drops slowly, indicating that the change observed is in the wrong direction. The curve illustrated for "structure" shows first a drop, then a rise. For "procedure" there is a fast rise and an equally rapid drop, showing some progress that was not sustained. With respect to "rate," the individual does poorly all along, and the data above this grid show almost complete agreement that this trainee's pace is too rapid.

If we look at the bottom grid we see that the "overall" rating, from session to session, has improved from about "3½" (or average) to about "5½." (This is an absolute score.)

Were this the summary chart of a specific individual, he or she would learn that while there are improvements in the areas of control, attitude, and emphasis, there still are problems in terms of relations, procedure, and rate.

While the terms should be self-descriptive, it may be wise—if this system is used—for the role-play facilitator and the participants to go over these forms and attempt to agree on their meanings so that some consistency is obtained. Usually, there is little difficulty in understanding them.

ROLE-PLAYER RATING SHEET

Directions:
1. On each of the nine scales, circle the dot that represents your opinion of what the role player did.
2. Underline the dot that represents your opinion of what should have been done.
3. If what was done and what should have been done are the same, the same dot will be circled and underlined.
4. There is no "good" or "bad" end on the first nine scales. Whether one should be flexible or firm, etc., depends on the situation.
5. The difference between the circled and the underlined dot represents the "error" of that factor in that situation.
6. Circle one dot of the overall rating to indicate your general reaction to the role player's effectiveness.

Role Player _____Observer _____

Situation _____

_____

_____Date _____

				Difference
Stand	Flexible	● ● ● ○ ● ● ●	Firm	( )
Control	Leader	● ● ● ○ ● ● ●	Subordinate	( )
Communication	Talk	● ● ● ○ ● ● ●	Listen	( )
Attitude	Tense	● ● ● ○ ● ● ●	Relaxed	( )
Emphasis	Person	● ● ● ○ ● ● ●	Problem	( )
Relations	Friendly	● ● ● ○ ● ● ●	Cold	( )
Structure	Formal	● ● ● ○ ● ● ●	Informal	( )
Procedure	Directive	● ● ● ○ ● ● ●	Non-directive	( )
Rate	Rapid	● ● ● ○ ● ● ●	Slow	( )

Overall Rating

Poor   ● ● ● ○ ● ● ●   Good

ROLE- PLAYER SUMMARY CHART

Directions:

1. This chart tells you how you are developing in terms of various be-havioral factors and in terms of your overall ratings.
2. Take all the Role-Player Rating Sheets that were completed about you for any session or situation and count the number of times you were rated "too flexible" (circles to the left of underlines). Put this number in the space after "flexible" at the top of the grid labeled "stand" on the summary chart.
3. Count the number of times you were rated "too firm" (circles to the right of underlines). Put this number after "firm."
4. Count the times the circles and underlines coincide and put this number after "O.K."
5. Do the same for the other grids.
6. When rated again do the same, putting new numbers after the old ones as shown in the example following.
7. Subtract the differences between the circles and underlines (maximum difference is six) and record the numbers found on the rating sheets for all factors.
8. For each factor, add these differences. Sum the differences for each factor and then divide by the number of raters. This number represents your "average error."
9. Place data on the grid of the summary chart in terms of the session and the "average error" as shown in the following example.
10. For "overall rating" merely add the ratings, from 1 to 7 (poor = 1, good = 7), average from the rating chart, and transfer the averages to the summary chart.

Name *Walt Logan*

Stand

Flexible 0110000100
Firm 6756 876 796
O.K. 2113102 102

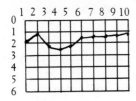

Control

Leader _____
Subordinate _____
O.K. _____

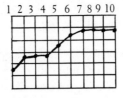

Communication

Talked _____
Listened _____
O.K. _____

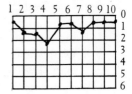

Attitude

Tense _____
Relaxed _____
O.K. _____

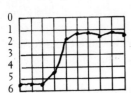

Emphasis

Person _____
Problem _____
O.K. _____

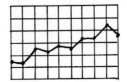

Relations

Friendly _____
Cold _____
O.K. _____

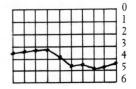

Structure

Formal _____
Informal _____
O.K. _____

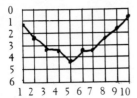

Procedure

Directive _____
Non-directive _____
O.K. _____

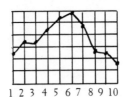

Rate

Rapid 885 7877867
Slow 0001000000
O.K. 0021/01031

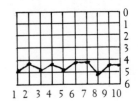

Overall

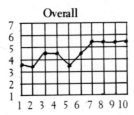